# EXTRAORDINARY JOURNEYS OF
# ORDINARY WOMEN

## COMPILED BY
## SHARON SINGLETON

authorHOUSE®

*AuthorHouse™*
*1663 Liberty Drive*
*Bloomington, IN 47403*
*www.authorhouse.com*
*Phone: 1-800-839-8640*

*First published by AuthorHouse 7/20/2009*

*ISBN: 978-1-4389-9820-6 (e)*
*ISBN: 978-1-4389-9819-0 (sc)*

*Printed in the United States of America*
*Bloomington, Indiana*

*This book is printed on acid-free paper.*

# Read about the exciting 'journeys' of these ladies

**Sharon Singleton**- Resides in Claremont, Ca. and has the great honor of knowing each of these women and the incredible stories that are shared in this book

**Millie Bollback** – Married to Harry Bollback, Co-director of Word of Life, Scroon Lake, New York, What an exciting life! From the jungles of Brazil to opening Word of Life ministries in over 55 countries!

**Gerda Hilda (Baumann) Kuykendall** – Incredible life story of a girl born in Germany during the time that Adolf Hitler was in power.

**Judy Shoff** – Pastors wife for 51 years. Very active with Women's Ministries and African Inland Missions International, now after 'retiring', is very active with Titus Ministries and Christian Ministries Training Assoc. of Los Angeles

**Lillie Knauls** – Touring with the Bill Gaither Trio, Singing & preaching about the love of God in 57 countries

**Jacquelyn Havens** – From a family of fourteen children, Ladies Bible Class Teacher, Palm Desert, Ca., Attended Wheaton College & Baylor University

**Yrena M. Friedman** – Pharmacist for twenty-five years and speaker for Christian Women's Clubs in So. California came from family that went through the holocaust, now lives in San Diego, Ca.

**Judy De Young** – Married to Jimmy De Young. Resided in Jerusalem for 12 years, where they weathered 39 Scud attacks. Now working with Day of Discovery television program and Prophecy Today radio and internet reports from the Middle East heard on over 800 stations.

**Ruth Kamena** – From a background of witchcraft to a glorious change of life.

**Bonnie Carlton** – Attended Buffalo Bible Institute, Taught women and children through Grace Mission, in Haiti.

**Wanda Lewark** – In 2005 was appointed by the Virginia Governor to a position on the Motor Vehicle Dealer Board. She was also named as the first woman National Quality Dealer – the highest honor that industry gives.

**Julia Fries** – Looking at her life in terms of seasons, followed God's leading to many places all over the world with International Teams. Retire? No! Instead went to work with Rawhide Boys Ranch in Wisconsin.

**Bobbie Garland** – Outstanding story of overcoming pain and sorrow during which time she wrote the poem titled "My Lament".

**Sheila Colclasure** – Non-Hodgkins Lymphoma.........What? Now living in Texas, Sheila tells of her battle not only with cancer but finding out that her husband had his own battle to face with sexual addiction.

**Marylin D. Blair** – Living in Maryland she is President of her own company and recipient of numerous awards

**Pauline Grant** – Taught in elementary schools and developed a ground breaking phonics program called Alphabet Noodle Factory that became a standard in the Glendora,Ca school districts and throughout schools in Southern California. She received the Glendora Reading Teacher of the Year Award in 1990 and became Azusa Pacific Universities student teacher mentor in l994.

**Della Albright** – The Prodigal Daughter, a story of family prayers answered.

**Donna Adams** – Pastors wife and teacher for many, many Bible classes in California and Payson, Arizona

**Lynne Castle** – Handles finances at a family law firm but her strongest desire was always to be a mom.

**Myrna Tuckley** – Internationally renowned for her fashion trend predictions and world wide President of her trade association. Corporate Color Consultant & National Spokesperson

# INTRODUCTION

Several years ago a friend gave me a book that made such an impact on my life that over the years I've thought about it over and over. It was the life stories of many different well known women and what God had done in their lives. The only problem with the book was that many of the women had not yet reached the 'golden years' and we had no way of knowing how their lives had really turned out.

When gathering the stories for this book, one thing is very clear. Most of us are not celebrities that have a great number of people that know us, BUT each woman is of great value in God's eyes and has been given her own life story and not two of the stories are the same. Sometimes we wish we could have a "do over" but when God made us, He gave us the temperament and the experiences and backgrounds that we have, because He wanted someone just like us in the world right now!

I have been blessed with many wonderful friends with very powerful life journeys. Some you may know and others probably not. Each one brings me back to the God who is in control and cares about our every need. When I thought about each of these ladies, God put on my heart that these life journeys needed to be shared.

I pray that as you read the journeys of these extraordinary ladies, that you will cry and laugh and relate, but most of all that you will see in each journey that our God is a God of hope, a God of second chances and that your own story could be a blessing to others also.

God wants to make our life an impact and our supreme desire should be to know God and to make Him known to others……..family, friends, neighbors and people you may meet only once.

The women in this book have shared the good, bad, blessings and disappointments that they have gone through in obedience to following God's path for their lives. Did they ever get off of that path? Which one of us hasn't?.........Their stories are all so different and yet have one common thread tying them all together. It is their love for Jesus Christ and a strong desire to walk with Him in obedience to God's word.

As you read about these ladies, think about your own journey through life and how God set you on that path. Think about the impact that your life has made in the lives of others around you. Where were you born? What was your family life like? What were the circumstances that lead you into a personal relationship with Jesus Christ? How has that impacted your life? Would you feel free and willing to share your journey through life with others?

The scriptures tell us that "All the days ordained for me were written in your book before one of them came to be." It is my hope that you enjoy reading these stories as much as I have and that you may even be encouraged to write down your own life story and share it with others ........or with me. You can send your story to Sharon Singleton and my e-mail address is sms21be@aol.com I would love to hear from you!

Sharon Singleton has the incredible ability to weave together a fascinating and inspirational collection of life stories that will keep you engrossed in the pages of this book. What better way to grow in your faith than to read the stories of 21st Century women as they journey through life. You will find yourself hidden in the pages of this book. I have been blessed to know and watch the author in her own life-journey as she has interacted with the ordinary women whose lives have been anything but ordinary.

Jimmy DeYoung, Day of Discovery & Prophecy Today

# DEDICATION

To my daughter Jan who has truly been a gift from God, she is an enthusiastic witness for Jesus plus having the gentle heart of a peacemaker. Just knowing a person like you is special, but having you for a daughter is something I will be eternally grateful for. You are well on your path to discovering your EXTRAORDINARY JOURNEY

# MY STORY (Sharon Singleton)
# ONE REGRET

For weeks I had thought about whether to include my own life's story in this book. As I spoke with one of the other writers I mentioned this fact to her. I told her that my life's journey is a little 'spicy'. Her answer was "So was King David's and many others in the Bible but God did not leave that part of their stories out." As a matter of fact it is their vulnerability that is the very thing so many of us can relate to.

So here is my story...........

I was raised in a wonderful Christian family. My Mom and Dad were very hard working people who put God first in everything they did and it was reflected in the lives they lived. Dad was a Bible teacher and song leader at church along with working in his secular job and Mom worked hard at everything.......from taking care of four children and being the best cook ever, to having part time jobs to help out with expenses that raising four kids involved. Church life was important to our family. We attended Sunday morning and evening services and also Wednesday night Bible studies. I came to an understanding faith in Jesus Christ at the age of ten.

I attended Christian schools until junior high and life seemed great! My life was very sheltered. I said sheltered, not pampered! We were far from wealthy, but until high school that really didn't matter to me. We had great times together, both at home and at church, plus having such a large extended family, feeling lonely was almost impossible.

Going into high school things changed.

My parents went through some very hard times, the family business failed and even putting food on the table became a daily challenge. They had to file for bankruptcy. That was hard on everyone in our family and for the first time made me very aware that the girls at the new public school that I now attended seemed to have so much and I had so little. One red skirt and white blouse one 'hand-me-down' dress and one other dress barrowed from my mom........and not much more. Dad and Mom worked very hard and eventually paid back (with interest) everyone from the bankruptcy, something most people never do, but what an example to the four of us kids. God blessed them and gave them very special times together before they went home to be with Him. Doing what would be right before God was always taught in our home.

After graduation, I went to work for Sears plus started attending the college department at the First Baptist Church. My older brother had been going there so I got to know a lot of his friends and fit in very easily. Those were wonderful times. Sip and Sings on Sunday nights were at different homes, plus Bible studies, beach parties and all the other fun things that were planned for us. There were a couple hundred young adults attending and something always going on. In addition each year we had College Briefing Conferences at Forest Home Christian Conference Center in the San Bernardino Mountains.........It was a blast and my life was once again very happy!

One particular Sunday I noticed a new guy in our class. He had graduated from a State University and so was a bit older than most of us. That Sunday he was up front giving his testimony of how he had come to know the Lord and how hard his life had been since childhood. His story brought the class to tears and I remember saying to God "he only needs someone to really love him".

Some time passed and I was going on with my life, when I got a phone call from 'this guy'. He asked me if I would like a job at the company he was working for and since he was in the Personnel Department he could hire me if I passed a typing test. I told him that I hadn't been around a typewriter in a couple of years and probably couldn't do much with one anymore, but he said to come in anyway. He told me that he would let me practice and then give me the test. He led me into a room and told me to practice, but when he came back he said "that was your test and you failed it". However, God had something different in mind and at that very moment one of the managers came through the door and asked who I was. He was told that I hadn't passed my test. The manager told 'the guy' to hire me anyway, and that his secretary would teach me anything I needed to know. So, I was hired!

'The guy' and I got into a car pool with a couple other people from work, got to liking each other and soon began dating. What should have been a happy time instead turned into some of the darkest days of my life.

The one and only time I was intimate with someone, ended in finding out that I was pregnant. In today's world the girls are taught that being pregnant outside of marriage is 'no big deal', but over forty years ago it was a huge tragedy. My parents were so ashamed of me and didn't hold back from letting me know how much I had hurt and disappointed them. I went on to work after finding this out, but soon discovered I couldn't be at work either. Couldn't concentrate or do much of anything but cry. I finally decided the best thing to do was tell 'the guy' as soon as possible.

Many from the college department at church were attending the summer College Briefing Conference and I knew he had gone up there for the week. I decided to drive up to the mountains to tell him the news. If I had expected comfort and love from someone that had told me he loved me so many times, it all went up in smoke when I found him as he was already with another girl. My heart sank as I saw how quickly he had turned to someone else. I told him that I had something to discuss with him, he told me to go wait for him to come to me. I waited.........., when he eventually came I told him that the doctor had just told me that I was pregnant. His response was something I will never forget. He told me that he would give me some money and to go away and have an abortion. Up to that point in my life I didn't know it was even possible to feel that alone. For a fleeting moment I thought about the suggestion of abortion but this was a baby, our baby, someone God loved and someone I would get to know and love. The trip back down the mountain is pretty much of a blur, only many tears. Abortion was something I would never choose and not an option for me but I had no answers as to where I would go from there.

When Jesus said "I will never leave you or forsake you", He is the one you can always count on. As I look back after this many years, He was always there guiding and guarding me as I took many unknown steps.

A few days later we finally had a chance to sit down and talk about what had happened. After advice and counseling from so many, we finally decided the right thing to do was to get married. The worst part of this decision was the fact that he decided after the wedding that he should have married his old girlfriend. He told me of his 'undying love' for her constantly. He played a record she had given him every night and talked about her everyday.

At seven months into the pregnancy, the doctor informed me that we were going to have twins. My husband finally stopped talking about his old girlfriend and started caring a little about me.

God blessed us with two beautiful babies, a boy and a girl, a blue eyed blond and a brown eyed brunette. They were and still are precious! (Although I'm not sure they would care for that description at this age.) Thirteen months later we were blessed with another wonderful baby boy and our family started coming together.

Three years into the marriage my husband decided to accept a job in Florida, three thousand miles away from home. That was the first of nineteen moves, many from coast to coast.

We moved and moved, had beautiful homes and met some of the dearest people God ever put on this planet. I got involved in singing for the churches we attended and working with Christian Women's Clubs, plus taking the kids to all the activities the kids were involved in while my husband would teach Bible classes. That part of my life was very special to me as I met such dear friends that continue to be close to this very day. It has been said that if you have one or two close friends in your life you are blessed.....I can just say I've been abundantly blessed in that department!

The part I didn't know until years later was that my husband had secretly made a vow to leave when the youngest of our kids turned eighteen.

Eleven years into our marriage came the second major turn in my life. We had just uprooted from Long Island, New York and moved back to California, and since singing had been such a large part of my life I started looking for another opportunity to start singing again. I joined a mixed quartet and we traveled locally singing for churches in the So. California area. I loved it! The harmony was beautiful and it was exciting meeting so many new people all the time. The turn came when I got involved with one of the singers. He told me that he loved me and I fell very hard for him. My husband had never said those words to me except before we were married and I longed to have someone love me and be able to give love in return. I called it love.........the Bible calls it sin and it is forbidden. Oh yes there is pleasure in sin for a season and it is extremely hard to walk away from but a moment of pleasure can bring a lifetime of heartache.

When my husband came home from a business trip he told me that during that same time God had given him a dream that he was going to loose me and for the first time, knew he didn't want that to happen. We sat down and talked and I told him what had been happening in my life and asked for his forgiveness. I must say at this point that his forgiveness was only in words. What happened had been such a shock to him, that for years after, he told anyone that would listen what I had done, plus adding a lot that I hadn't done.

My husband asked his foster mom to come over from Arizona and talk to me. She was a good, solid Bible believing woman that really lived her faith. Her life was one that showed in practical ways the love of Jesus to others. We talked for hours and hours. I was so confused. I didn't want to give up this new relationship, it seemed so loving and so hard to let go of. She helped me to see that as a Christian my choice was not between this new man in my life and my husband, it was between doing what I wanted and doing what God wanted me to do. The choice was clear. I got down on my knees and prayed, I told the Lord that at any cost I wanted His will for my life. The next day I put an end to our relationship and even our friendship, made a promise to never see him again and though it was extremely hard, I kept that promise.

This same dear friend showed me Isaiah 54:4 to the end of the chapter which seemed to be my life on paper. I clung to those verses of love from the Lord Jesus. He would be 'my husband', my protector, my defender and so much more. He is the one I talk to, listen to and walk with daily. Learning all of this, I have one regret. I wish I could write my life's story with no sin, no wrong choices, and no disappointing others as the story of my life, but that wouldn't be true to the way it was. When reading about many people in God's word, He didn't leave out the sin that had been in their lives and just tell the good things. Instead there is much emphasis on the grace and mercy of a loving God when repentance and restoration are involved. If only we could learn to forgive the way that God loves and forgives us.

After a few months, my husband decided to keep climbing the corporate ladder, and we moved another three thousand miles again, this time to Maryland. We moved three more times in Maryland, constantly fixing up houses or building a new one. We ended our time there in a beautiful house, seven thousand square foot English Tudor sitting on top of a hill overlooking a golf course and country club. The view was beautiful, but inside we were falling apart.

By this time our kids had turned eighteen and my husband decided to start looking around for someone new. It didn't take long as he was near the top of his profession and that seems very attractive to women looking for security. He remarried about two months after our divorce was final.

Looking back even after going through some hard times, I can thank the Lord from the bottom of my heart for all the growth that came into my life during this time. Growth that was very hard to go through, more moves around the country and more turmoil in the family than I ever wanted, especially for our kids, but in the book of

James chapter 1:2-5 the scriptures say "Dear brothers and sisters, whenever trouble comes your way, let it be an opportunity for joy. For when your faith is tested, your endurance has a chance to grow. So let it grow, for when your endurance is fully developed, you will be strong in character and ready for anything." The Lord was giving me opportunities that I would have never had and growth that probably wouldn't have happened just staying in one town. That plan, now unveiled to me seems so worth any hurt that has taken place.

What I am not suggesting is that growth only comes after a result of sin…….but am forever thankful that a loving God does not just write us off as unusable, but forgives and uses us to share the gospel with others if we are truly repentant .

For instance, our move to Virginia………we were in a great neighborhood with wonderful people that until that time did not know the Lord. There were three women in particular that have made such a difference in my life.

The first is Sara. She was a flight attendant and a model, very kind and just the sort of woman anyone would value for a friend. On a particular night she had a party for the people in the neighborhood, we attended but I had such a stiff neck that it was even hard to turn my head. Sara's husband offered some medication for my neck, I said thanks and that I would return it in a couple days. When I came back, Sara invited me in for coffee and some chit-chat, but the awesome part of it was two hours later when she prayed with me to receive Jesus Christ as her Lord and Savior. She attended a Bible study with me the following week and told everyone what had happened. A few years ago I received word that Sara had been killed in a car accident. My heart was full of grief for loosing a dear friend and at the same time so very thankful to God for letting me be a

8

part of His plan to bring her into His kingdom. I will see her again!

At that meeting was another neighbor that lived directly across the street from Sara, her name was Wanda. Sara told Wanda what had happened and wondered why Wanda (also a Christian) had never shared this good news with her. It was a real wake up call for Wanda who to this very day is one of the most loving, outspoken examples of a dedicated Christian that I have ever met plus being a very dear friend.

Another neighbor was Jo who lived right next door to me. She attended a liberal church but really did not know the Lord. We met for coffee at my house or hers after seeing the kids off to school most mornings. She says that I wouldn't leave her alone until she came to know the Lord which is probably true, but today along with being a nurse is a wonderful Sunday school teacher and through her life has shared the love of Jesus with many others. See how the Lord worked all things for my good and His glory!!!!! What a blessing!!

There are many other stories that I could share from most of the places we lived that would never have been possible had I not been willing to do things God's way instead of my own. This was God's calling for my life to be able to not only live it but at this stage in my life to share it through this book. This is a blessing that I never anticipated.

We were divorced in 1981. The years that followed were equally hard but in a different way. Since we had lived away from my home state for so many years, I wanted to move back to be near my parents and spend some time with them. Our kids were away at college and were busy with their studies so I packed up and made the move. I found a small house to rent and tried to just 'mellow-out' from all that had transpired. I thought it would be nice to spend some time with my mom and sister, doing lunch, shopping etc., but that only happened once before my mom had her first major stroke.

The next nine years were spent taking care of Mom and Dad. Mom had two major strokes and could do nothing for herself. It was very hard for both my dad and me as she was at home all of that time, (not in a convalescent home). After Mom went home to be with the Lord, my Dad found out that he had cancer and for the next two years I stayed very close to him and helped until in 2001 he also went to Heaven. During this time I also got my real estate license and have been in that business for over twelve years.

While all of this was going on, our 'kids' turned into young adults and finished college. Our youngest son also graduated from Dallas Theological Seminary and became a pastor of a fast growing church in North Carolina. Children are truly a blessing from the Lord and I feel very blessed to have the three wonderful adult children that I have. They have all married wonderful mates and have given me five beautiful (and smart) grandchildren. They are all consistently sharing their faith in Jesus Christ with others. If that sounds like a happy Mom and Grandmom......you're right!!

Almost two years ago my doctor called with the news that I also had cancer. At the time it seemed overwhelming and yet looking back the Lord was with me every minute of every day, along with friends and family. At last report everything is just fine. During that time the Lord gave me a promise that I cling to. It is found in 1Peter 5:10 "And after you have suffered for a little while, the God of all grace...will Himself perfect, confirm, strengthen and establish you." What a comfort, to know that I am in God's care, and that even at this point in my life God still had some surprises for me.

With a promise like that I can honestly say that I'm looking forward to these 'golden years.'

Reflecting on life and the story of my own journey, I got the idea that hearing about the journeys of other ladies would be very interesting also. In the book of Psalms, chapter 139:16b, the scriptures say "all the days ordained for me were written in your book before one of them came to be." It's awesome to read of the differences in the journeys of so many women that came through searching, trials, heartaches and joy to a place of anticipating the 'what's next?' and knowing that a loving God will be right here with us. I hope that you enjoy reading the 'journeys' of these women as much as I have and that you may even be encouraged to write your own story and possibly share it with others or with me.

# MY STORY.....MILLIE BOLLBACK

This is the story of my life. I was glad that I was born but what really made the difference in my life was when I married my husband, the incredible man HARRY BOLLBACK !!!!!...and that is true!

The story of my life begins in Bloomfield NJ. in September of 1927....the beginning years of the Great Depression. It was a humble beginning. Home was on the third for flat of a two flat house. My mother turned the little 3rd floor, into HOME for us. My mother was a great believer of home and close family relationships, and poor as we were she instilled in us three girls that your family is the mainstay of your life. She had come from old American stock, dating back to the days of the early colonists who settled in what is now the great Essex County of NJ. Her family, the Condits, were huge land owners in that part of the state.

It grieved my mother that my father did not have a close relationship with his brothers. His family came from Germany, and I believe my grandparents met on the ship coming to the New World in the late 1800's. They married in 1894 and settled in the Newark area of NJ. Dad was born handicapped, but had a brilliant mind, and graduated from Bloomfield High School, "Most likely to succeed". However, as life went on for him, nothing could have been farther from the truth. He was a fun loving little guy, but all through my life I have believed that he never learned responsibility because of his handicap, a club foot, and the many surgeries he went through as a child. He married and unfortunately had no idea how to support a family, much less hold down a job for more than two or three months. His mother, my dear sweet grandmother, loved him dearly, and he could do no wrong in her eyes. I'm sure she never dreamed she was helping him to make poor decisions, and gave him no responsibilities, because of his foot. He also had 2 or 3 webbed fingers, and I'm sure this bothered her. As little kids we were over at her house often and played with our cousins. Daddy's family were heavy beer drinkers, and while the adults sat around and drank beer, we children were given the pretzels to eat, that always accompanied the beer. My father's family had a "good" standing in the town, and I'm sure that as my father got older and drank more, his brothers were ashamed of him, although they loved us children.....maybe they "felt sorry" for us.

When my parents married, my grandfather gave my parents that third floor flat to live in, rent free. All three of us girls were born in our home, for mother made life, in that little tiny apartment, home for us, and she always instilled upon us that a house doesn't make a home. You can make a home now matter where you live...be it one room, a tiny third floor flat (to mother's horror, she overheard some neighbors say, "Those Winkler girls live in the attic of that house"). My mother was very proud of her family heritage. She came from a very loving family of many spinster aunts and bachelor uncles, who all showered her with so much love. Mother just could not understand a family that did not love each other, consider, respect, honor, and do nice things for each other.

Mother loved people, and she always welcomed our friends and our family into our home. At this writing, I do not remember a time though, when any of my father's family came to visit us...we always went to their homes, and they always welcomed us, and we had fun with them. Mother's brothers and sister, and my grandparents came OFTEN to visit us, and we knew we were loved by them. The holidays were especially special, because they were always special to my mother in her family growing up, so Thanksgiving and Christmas were the greatest times of our lives. Mother knew just what to do to make those days wonderful and so memorable to us. Daddy, learned to "jump on the bandwagon", and always sat at the head of the table, and mother at the foot...Aunts, Uncles and cousins surrounded the table, and my grandmother and grandfather, Condit were very prominent at the table.

We always used the "good" dinnerware (probably given to us, or bought in Woolworth's or Grants) for these special occasions and on Sunday. They were SPECIAL, and we learned to value "special things". It was kind of like our Sunday clothes. We could wear our "Sunday dress" for Sunday school and church, and we could leave it on IF we put on an apron while we ate. The same went for our shoes. We had Sunday shoes (for dress) and any old shoes for everyday.

Daddy was never able to "hold down a job", so mother, to her great embarrassment went out and cleaned homes to be sure we had bread on the table. Holidays were different. I don't know where the money came from for Thanksgiving and Christmas. As we grew older, I really feel my father took to such heavy drinking, because he did love us, had no idea how to show it, and was absolutely frustrated with life.

When Dad's parents died, my father received a nice inheritance, and along with the money, we got the three flat house, also Grandma's electric refrigerator. We had an icebox up to that time, and bought the ice from an ice man that came down the street selling great huge squares of ice for people like us. We loved that because as little kids we would run down the street begging the iceman to give us a piece of ice...oh, how refreshing those little splinters of ice were on those hot days of summer. Well, we could have been "set" with all that we received upon my grandparent's death...BUT...

Daddy took to gambling now and played the chariot horses in Freehold, NJ. Between the heavy drinking and the arguing over the gambling, life became miserable at home with my family.  Daddy lost everything...the house, the money...everything.....He became like a man without a home, a family, love....

Now...something happened...Jesus came into our home....How did that happen??

When I was just in kindergarten, a wonderful family who loved the Lord moved into a house just down the street from us.  They didn't have much financially either, but Mrs. Schwanewede KNEW the Lord and she told us about how much He loved us.

Now, I have to say here, that once we were saved mother told us that she had received Jesus as her Savior as a young girl, but, I don't believe she ever had any discipling, and became an ordinary church goer. She took us to church and Sunday school as little girls, EVERY Sunday.  We didn't miss, unless we were sick. Sunday school and church became a very important part of our lives, and is for me, until this day. Mother also listened, without fail, to Christian Radio programs like The Young People's Church of the Air. Rev. Percy Crawford was the evangelist, from the Pocono's of Pennsylvania, and Dr. Charles E. Fuller's weekly broadcast from California. To hear these programs was like a ritual, every Sunday afternoon in our house....so the Gospel was being presented loud and clear, every week right in our living room.

In the meantime, Mrs. Schwanewede's daughter was my age and we became very best friends...from kindergarten until today...Elaine and I did everything together from kindergarten through our teen years. I think I used to "escape" from the sadness in our home to her's, when things got rough in mine.  I remember so well, laying my head on Mrs. Schwanewede's lap, and she would comfort me by just passing her hand over my brow. She also introduced me to my first cup of tea. She would explain the Gospel story graphically with "stick" figures...draw pictures of boys and girls arguing and fighting, punching each other, and then she drew a cross in the middle of the page, and then draw happy children, with smiles and joy on the other side of the cross. She would ask me what makes the difference? Then she told me that Jesus died for the naughty boys and girls, and if they believed on Him, and would trust Him as their Savior...He would come into their lives and change them...that His death on the cross was for EACH naughty girl and boy. She told me that I had to accept the fact that He died in my place for my sins, my naughtiness. He loved me so much that He, God's Son died for me. I don't remember accepting Jesus as my Lord and Savior at that time, but when I was 14, Rev. Percy Crawford had an evangelistic meeting in the Baptist church in my town. MY mother let my sisters and me go with Mrs. Schwanewede and her family. I don't remember if my mother went or not. But we were there.

When the invitation was given to receive Christ, my sister Ruth began to cry, and she sobbed, so much that a dear Christian lady got up from her pew and came over. Put her arms around my sister and asked if she wanted to receive Christ into her heart. Choking with tears Ruth went forward with her. MY attention was turned to myself...If Ruth felt she needed a savior, how much more I did...I was the middle child, in every argument, and defense of myself in the family. I was THE sinner, not Ruthie. She was too good....I got up and walked down the aisle to accept Jesus' death in my place! I was saved...born again! And God began to do His work in me.

During my teen years, our pastor introduced us to other Christian organizations outside our church. One was the Newark Evangelistic Committee. This organizations had many, and diverse activities to reach the youth of Newark and Essex County with the gospel. There were roller skating rallies, and always after skating there was a gospel message preached. Also, the Committee had FUN rallies where they rented a local gymnasium in a public school. They invited churches from all over Essex County to bring their youth groups, and for the young people to invite unsaved friends. Here we were led in all kinds of relay races and fun games...all these churches together, divided into teams, and we played, and got to know other Christian young people from our area.

At the same time Jack Wyrtzen began his Word of Life broadcast, with live broadcasts aired directly from the Gospel Tabernacle just around the corner from Times Sq. on 8th Av. and 42nd St. Our pastor took us as a group to those Sat. Night rallies. Here we saw many people come to Jesus. As we got a bit older and began to date, we went with the young people from church without our pastor. Between Jack's rallies and the Evangelistic Committees fun activities, we really had wonderful teen years getting to know Christian young people. The Evangelistic. Committee, also, started a Bible school on Friday nights in Newark which I attended. The examples set before me in the leadership of the roller-skating and fun nights were imprinted deep inside me, and I was learning, so much, just by the example of those young adults who led us. I owe so much of my Christian life to those dear people who lived the Christian life in front of me. At the same time, I was seeing young married Christian couples....how they lived, how they responded to each other, and the Lord set goals in my heart to have a happy Christian home. I wanted a life like they

17

had.  I wanted to be what they were....and God began to lead.

Our Pastor also encouraged us to go to another Baptist church...Brookdale Baptist, at the other end of town.  Pastor Anderson had "Above the Clouds" Christian broadcasts from his church each Sunday night at 9:00 PM.  Our whole youth group, maybe 5 to 15 of us would go up to the broadcast after our church service was over,  we had hymn sings in our homes after church, so we were gathered together as a group...Also "The Miracle Book Club" taught by one of the members of our church involved us....

When I was about 15 our Pastor took us to a Christian Camp in Lake Canandaigua, NY.  This was my first camping experience. It was WONDERFUL...a whole week of Bible teaching and fun.  I "ate it up".  During the campfire service, God really spoke to my heart... and I realized there were people looking at the same moon, who had never heard even the name of Jesus... God was beginning to speak to me about serving Him... ME, reaching out to others, not just all I could get for myself. I must have been a sophomore or junior in high school...but I knew God was leading me.

Into my senior year, I knew I had to go to Bible school and prepare for service to the Lord...but where and how?  There was no money in my family; I knew they could not help me financially. These were the 2nd World War years, and there wasn't much of anything to be found. Well, the War ended in 1945 just soon after I graduated from HS. I needed to earn some money so I could go to Bible School.  All during HS I baby-sat and became a "mother's helper" after school.  This helped me earn spending money, and for clothes.  But, you can well imagine that we lived on "hand me down" clothes from the time we were babies...even through HS.

18

After graduation, I got a job at the Prudential Life Insurance Co. in Newark. I was only there 6 months when I got a telephone call from a friend who had begun to work at Jack Wyrtzen's Word of Life Office in NYC. She told me they needed a receptionist, and did I want to apply for the job!!! Oh, what joy! I'd be doing God's work...serving Him in WOL Office, while I still saved my money to go to Bible School. They accepted me, and what an education I got...right there....I was scared to death...Jack Wyrtzen...I had to talk with him personally.

I was so intimidated, felt so insecure, and inadequate. I was not a secretary, but I was like their errand girl that picked up the mail, helped count offerings, and delivered them to the bank. I met so many people, leaders in God's work and the Lord was working on me. I learned what prayer was all about. We started each morning with prayer and devotions before we went into the office. Oh, how much I learned. God was dealing with me. I do remember talking with Norman Clayton, the great Christian song writer. He had written so many wonderful songs with words that reached deep down into my heart..."Now I Belong to Jesus, Jesus belongs to Me"...He was the organist for Jack's rallies, and traveled with him a lot in his evangelistic ministry, so he came into the office a lot. I remember telling him I didn't "have any testimony. I hadn't done so many wicked things so that my life was drastically changed". What would I ever say if Jack called on me to give a testimony? He told me I had a great testimony. God in His plan, for me, had kept me from this type of life, and I had no remaining scars on my body from my sin. Consequences from sin remain as scars, and I could praise him that the scars I had were borne on Jesus body on the cross. Oh, How I rejoice in the Lord, that He kept me from so much. My life was hid in Christ on the cross, and I became a new creature in Christ when I received Him...He took away all that childhood bitterness, and anger I had in my family. I had only received love at home, and I hadn't recognized it, and now I did. Thank you Lord.

I was 18 and working at WOL when Harry returned from the War...31/2 years serving as a Marine in the South Pacific. I had started working at WOL in early Jan. of 1946, and had applied to go to the old Providence Bible Institute in Providence, RI. I still didn't have enough money to go, but I was saving regularly. My salary was $21.00 a week, and if I remember correctly, my tuition for Providence was $200.00 a semester, and I still needed room and board...and now Harry, came into my life.....What was I going to do....? Well, to add to the dilemma, WOL had given me a week off to go to Lancaster to the big Missionary conference there. Pat, my girlfriend, at WOL, and I were going there for the week to serve tables, for the missionaries. They had meetings all day long...for a hundred or more of them... outsiders were invited to the huge evening missionary meetings, where the missionaries from all over the world gave their testimonies. During the day and at meals we were "thrown" together and were able to meet so many of the missionaries personally! What a privilege! Pat had read about the South American Indian Mission and was curious to know the missionaries who served there. We met and spent almost the entire week with their missionaries who served in the jungles of Brazil. How exciting! However, the very last night, a missionary was called upon to give his testimony. He was from Japan...this country had been our enemy! Our boys, just recently, were killed while fighting them...BUT, I heard loud and clear that God loved them, and he was there pleading for missionaries to go to reach them in

Japan. My heart was opened...was God speaking to me about going to Japan?

We returned to the office after our fabulous week at the mission's conf. I was still wondering about this "burden" on my heart, not only about Japan, but just serving the Lord overseas...Harry had come into my life...What about him? I liked him. I doubted that he had any intention of being a missionary....God is soooo good, Jack Wyrtzen noticed. He had scheduled a long trip down the East Coast of the US, and took Harry with him to play the piano. He not only had the meetings, but he also scheduled chapels in as many Christian colleges as he could find up and down the East Coast. He was praying for Harry. More than three years fighting a war has its consequences too, and Jack wanted to see Harry have a life totally committed to serve the Lord. Returning from that trip, when the invitation was given for commitment to serve the Lord, Harry stood right up and walked away from the piano to the front of the auditorium. He was committing his life to serve the Lord anywhere.

Right soon after that Ernie and Leona Lubkemann came into the office with their two little boys. Jack's secretary was Ernie's sister, and she had asked them to come in and meet the girls in the office. Ernie and Leona were missionaries with the South America Indian Mission, and had just returned on their first furlough from serving the Lord in the jungles of Brazil. The same country and mission the missionaries we had met in Lancaster were affiliated with. Hmmmmm... Harry happened to be in the office that afternoon, and he had known Erin, soon after Ernie had gotten saved and went to Bible College. During the war, Ernie and Leona were in Brazil, and NOW, we, Harry and I, were hearing their stories and experiences...How wonderfully the Lord leads, giving one a burden for many places when

He actually is leading you to one definite place. The field is the world. Well, after all this you can imagine... things began to develop between Harry and me and we recognized that God had given us a love for each other and He was not only leading us together, but to the Indians of Brazil.

Our sights were set. We decided it best for me to continue as God had led me to the Providence Bible Institute, and Harry applied for the old Philadelphia School of the Bible (now Philadelphia Biblical University). We felt we would get more out of our studies if we did not attend the same school. Harry gave me my ring and we were engaged in my home the night before Harry left for registration at PSOB. My mother, and father, had invited all our youth group to a turkey dinner...a farewell, for many of us leaving for preparation in many different schools to serve the Lord. Out of our youth group of maybe 15 or so, I think 5 or 6, maybe more went off to Bible School that year or the next. Pastor Jones, Mr. and Mrs. Harold Wentworth of the Newark Evangelistic Committee, Jack Wyrtzen, Dr. Anderson of Brookdale Baptist church...all your efforts to reach and disciple all our young people...me... those years, paid off. Thank you Lord for putting these people into my life...aside from MANY others whose Godly examples I follow to this day.

After our first year at the different Bible schools, we were married in first Baptist Church of Bloomfield, NJ with my pastor, Dr. Russell G Jones, and Jack Wyrtzen officiating. Norman Clayton played the organ, and Dr. Clayton Booth sang. Clayton Booth was the song leader for Jack Wyrtzen's early Word of Life Rallies.

While we were in Bible School, which by the way, the Lord provided my tuition from some Christian friends who did not want to make themselves known...isn't that great? Humble people, not proud of what they could do. I learned this from them too....let the Lord work His work through me and the whole world doesn't have to know who did what. At school I was able to get employment and able to pay the rest of my bills. God is so good. He takes care of His own.

While we were separated and at Bible school, I got a letter from Harry, he suggested writing our names and using the verse Joshua 1:9 as our life verse..."Have not I commanded thee, be strong and of good courage, be not afraid, neither be thou dismayed: , for the Lord thy God is with thee whithersoever thou goest") It was engraved in our wedding rings...and so it is...58 years later and you can still read Joshua 1:9....How God has used THAT verse in our lives. He truly gave it to us as a promise of His that we could depend upon Him for all our days. Thank God for His word.

Well, we took Wycliffe Bible translators Summer Inst. of Linguistics program in Norman, Oklahoma the summer of 1950, had been accepted by the South America Indian Mission (now known as SAM), and Harry had graduated from Philadelphia School of the Bible, that June We had a little girl, Linda, just one year old when we sailed out of NYC for Santos, Brazil (the port city for Sao Paulo), in Dec. of 1950. So MUCH had happened so fast for us that year of 1950...beside all the above we traveled so much in the Fall raising support, but basically our support came from Word of Life. Word of Life did not have any overseas ministries at that time, but supported many missionaries under other mission boards, and we were one of them. Many Christian friends stood behind us in adding to the support WOL had given.

We arrived in Santos by ship, and we were met by a man who was a relative of a believer in our church. This man was not a believer, but he became a good friend to us. He worked for an American Pharmaceutical company in Brazil, and supplied us with all the malaria medicine we needed, plus all other kinds of regular pharmaceutical supplies to use with the Indians...God provides!

We studied Portuguese in the city of Cuiaba, the capital of the State of Mato Grosso. While studying the language, we had the opportunity to visit the Paranatinga Mission station, where we would eventually be living among the Bakari Indians. This was a semi civilized tribe, and we were able to eventually make our home two miles from their village. We traveled by horseback...I carried Linda, now 21/2 years old, behind me on my horse, and we now had Larry, 4 months old when we moved out there) Harry carried him in his arms. Our house had been constructed by missionaries who lived there before us...walls were made of cow manure and sand....mixed, and then plastered over standing branches that encircled an area for the dirt floor. This gave us walls and we were able to whitewash it and even hang pictures!

We had a wood stove in the kitchen. The ceiling in the kitchen was very low and was made of grass...very hot in there. Our floors were all of dirt, and we were able to have different rooms in the house...no bathroom, just an outhouse out back....both missionary couples used the same outhouse...two doors..."Him" and "Her"....and Harold Reimer, a single missionary who came down to work with us. He had been on the WOL Camp staff.

Life there at the Paranatinga was quiet and nice. I really loved living out there, we had a few cows, missionaries had bought them before we came, and they had now left, so Harry learned to milk them, and also to shoe horses, and I learned to make cheese and dry meat in the sun - with Harry's help. Having all the cattle, we were able to butcher one for fresh meat, also dried a lot and gave a lot to the Indians. For entertainment we would all go out as a family, in the setting sun and watch the cows come in to be milked... Sunsets out there under the great big sky were fabulous. We walked in the rain. (Have you ever done THAT, for fun??? It is fun, when you don't mind getting wet, and you feel the heavy rain pounding on your back! We had no clothes dryer to put your wet clothes into, but that doesn't matter. Not long after the rain, the bright HOT sun comes out, and we just laid our clothes out on the bushes, or barbed wire fence to dry...and they steamed in the heat! Harry loved taking the children out to find wild flowers and bring them home to Mommy. We read Bible stories and nursery rhymes in books we had brought from the States. We had a refrigerator that we shared with the other missionary family, Tom and Betty Young...six months in our house and then we moved it to theirs for six months. When they left and another couple came, they came with a refrigerator, so the other one came back to us and we had it in our home until we left for furlough. The Youngs had two boys, Tommy and Jimmy, just older than our children, so they had a lot of fun together. After they left the station to live in Cuiaba, another couple, Bob and Pat Brian came...They had an old model T Ford...We didn't use it on the station because no place to buy gas, but they were able to use it for the three day trip to the nearest city...Cuiaba, maybe once in the 46 months or so, that they lived out there with me.

As my mother had taught us as children, it doesn't take a house to make a home...home is where your family and love is...no matter how big or how small YOU can make a home, and not even if it has dirt floors and cow manure and sand plastered wall....and that little crooked house, that smelled of cow manure...when it rained a lot...was HOME, and we loved it. Some of our furniture was made out of boxes covered with fabric... there was no screen or glass on the open windows, so we didn't have to worry about washing windows... We had wood shutters on each window, so we did have to be sure the shutters were close when the rain came down hard....as it did so often.

No electricity, so we had kerosene lanterns which we hung from the ceiling like a chandelier, and also had others that we just set around the room on cloth covered boxes that made great end tables.

We did purchase a simple dining room set while we were in language study in Cuiaba, and also a bed for us and a bed for Linda. We had a crib for Larry that was supposed to be bug and mosquito proof...The screen covered the crib all the way around, and even across the top. We brought it with us from the US for Linda, It was called a Kiddie Koop, and served us pretty well, BUT, the army ants did get in one or two times and we had to rescue our screaming baby boy, from the pinching of all those thousands of ants. I don't remember if those ants had poisonous bites, but I think it was the great number of them pinching all at one time that could literally make a person, or chicken, go "beside themselves"...and yes, they did get into the chicken coop, and many was the time when we had to go out and rescue the chickens from the ants in the dark...the old fashioned FLIT can (similar to OFF, in today's market) did the trick...Now, God did make the army ants good for something...they literally cleaned out the grass roof from all kinds of spiders, lizards, etc., and THAT was good...Good if you could move out of your house while they were there!!

We always set the table and ate around the table for three meals a day. Harold Reimer, our single missionary, joined us in our home for meals and ate with Tom and Betty for others. Harold had a guitar, which he used to like to strum and sing as he sat around in our living room. Harry had a little pump organ...and would you believe it, he wrote some gorgeous music on that little thing. I don't know if it had four octaves....worse than all that we saved it, and then LOST the manuscripts when we came to the US...somewhere...somehow....I used to feel so sorry for him...such big hands and strong fingers, and only that one little tiny instrument to play on...BUT, let me tell you that instrument was much used to reach the Indians....and we taught them to sing...even did a Christmas pageant with them...or tried to...only to have the three wisemen walk in the opposite direction of the star!!! We even tried an Easter sunrise service with them...the Bakiris...I don't know if they ever got to really understand what we were trying to teach them...the resurrection...God knows and we sowed the seed...

So that was living for us.  This is where our home was and where I stayed with the children and Betty Young and her children while our husbands and Harold went down river to minister to the Indian tribes. The only way to them was by dug out canoe, and the Youngs tried to go back every two years, but the trip was treacherous... no airstrips down there, and the trip had to be made when the rivers were fairly high. It was on one of these trips that the guys met the Chevante Indians.  Indians Tom had been praying for, for years, and a way to reach them.

The day came when the planned trip was ready and it was time to say goodbye.  Where were they going? Down an unexplored river...Was there communication with us? None, no cell phones, no mail, no computers in those days. They went and we all cried our tears as we said goodbye...trying to be brave. And you know what? We were brave.  The Lord made all of us courageous, and He literally took away fear from us as we said good bye. I don't think we stopped to think what was engraved in our wedding rings." Have not I commanded you, be strong and of good courage, be not afraid nor

dismayed, for the Lord is with thee wherever you go..."
Yessssss He said it, and He performed it in us...and the
days went on...just as they did when the men were with
us. Their return is another great story...how exciting it
was...and I believe all that has been recorded in the
book When the Arrow Flies" by Cunningham I must say
this, that my mouth fell wide open when they shared
their experiences they'd had with the Chevanti. I had
had no idea that they would encounter wild Indians who
literally tried to kill them, much less ride out the terrible
rapids in the rivers that could have taken their lives as
well...but God spared these men. He had other things
for them to do. The exciting thing that God did was
to bring these very Chevanti men almost to the door
of our house. It was about six months after our men
returned that a whole group of Chevanti men came.
After spending a day with us, eating wild mandioca (a
root similar to potato) talking with us...sign language
style. No weapons were with them, we knew they
wanted to be friends.  That day was the only day I had
contact with them until we returned to their village,
some 50 years later...just two years ago. So much has
happened in these years. There are now many churches
among them.  Missionaries from South America Indian
Mission had moved in and really taught them the Word
of God, and how to use it.  Last year they received the
Bible, at least the New Testament in their own language.
Wycliffe Bible translator missionaries had spent years
translating the Word for them, and NOW they have it.
Such rejoicing.  Also, many of the Indians have studied
at SAM's school near Cuiaba, others have gone to
Aquidauana and studied with the educated in the word,
Terena Indians.  The Chevanti has a thirst for the Word
of God.  Praise His name. How grateful we are that the
Lord was able to use us to find and show them the love
of God.  They accepted that love, came to Christ in

28

great numbers, and now after all these years they are becoming established, and have many many churches. In a recent missionary conf. that SAM had for Indian workers, the largest numbers present were Chevantis. AND, there are no foreign missionaries. They are the pastors and missionaries...

After all that, those wonderful years, we returned to the US and then returned to Brazil to start the first Word of Life Camp overseas. What experiences we had there near the city of Atibaia, about 35 miles out of Sao Paulo. We found the camp site, a beautiful valley with low mountains all around it. It was like a little cup...down in the valley. The kids soon called it the Enchanted Valley, and my how God has blessed that camping ministry. There was nothing like it...Brazilians hardly knew what camping was, much less a Bible conference thrown in with it. The valley exploded with exciting kids...hungry for the Word of God. When we weren't out at camp we lived in Sao Paulo, By this time we had three children, and then our youngest was born during our second year with Word of Life in Brazil.

Life, or living, in Sao Paulo, wasn't much different than living in the States...except at that time to have a telephone in the house was an expense we could not afford. Even when WOL got an office down town (center city) we rented a corner of a lawyer's office and were able to use his phone. We got a Brazilian secretary for the ministry soon after we arrived there. What an asset she was to us. She had church contacts everywhere in the city, and out. She was able to do scheduling for Harry and Harold's evangelistic campaigns. They wanted to be busy and they were. Meetings were set up all over Brazil. The guys, Harry and Harold, got a blue and white Willy's jeep and they drove it, with the Hammond organ in the back, and the Leslie speaker standing upright on the tailgate at the back of the jeep.

We didn't have enough money to purchase a tarp to cover it, in case of rain, so the guys took an old pink shower curtain and covered the speaker with it, and off they went...The schedule was - two weeks out on evangelistic meetings and two weeks at home. We did that for several years. The Reimer family and ours was like one family.

For all the years that we lived in Sao Paulo, Harold and Debora Reimer and their children lived very close to us. We really were like one big happy family. Our husbands really were of one mind and one purpose, serving the Lord. Debora was Brazilian, and never once did she say to me, "Millie, we do it this way in Brazil", yet I learned so much from her. She was so content with whatever she had, and took very good care of all that she had. She did not take for granted all that God provided her with. She was such a wise friend. We did everything together. We didn't have the jeep too long, when Harold felt he needed a better vehicle to drive the long distances, so they got a Volkswagen Combee, or van. How useful that vehicle was to all of us. Many times, after the guys had been away, the day was nice and they'd drive up and say ""let's go to Santos"...the beach!!! So all the kids, their five and our four would all pile in and off we would go...singing all the way.

Our children started their school years by going to a little private kindergarten and first grade that was just up the street from where we lived. Linda was getting older and we knew we had to do something about school. There were many other missionary families living in Sao Paulo from many different mission boards and we all had the same need - a school for our children. I don't know how the other missionary families felt, but Brazilian school seemed out of the question for our family. Brazilians had school six days a week, and varied school hours, sometimes into the evening hours. I really didn't like this system because of Harry's traveling. We knew that something had to be done, so along with several other missionary families we started, together, The Pan American Christian Academy. This turned out to be a wonderful school, and our children loved it. I believe that because of that school, so many of the missionary kids who were enrolled there have returned to Brazil, or gone other places around the world to serve the Lord. Few, if any, resented the fact that their parents were missionaries.

Often Harry and Harold tried to be home to go to church and Sunday School with us, and that was great because I believe the children saw that we believed in family worship. On Sunday nights, meetings were often scheduled in the city area, and sometimes we were able to take the children with us.

We tried to involve the older children, Linda and Larry into the ministry as much as possible. Linda helped in the kitchen at camp, and Larry often went with his dad to local street meetings, and helped pass out tracts, etc.

At home, we had child evangelism Bible classes for Brazilian children in our neighborhood once a week, and I was able to do a weekly Bible study in the public schools under the auspices of Child Evangelism Fellowship.

The work of Word of Life in Brazil seemed to explode like the atom bomb. It was just so widely accepted by the evangelical church in that great country. They'd had nothing like it in their great country. The evangelistic campaigns, the camps, and then the radio carried the Gospel, of the Lord Jesus all over the country. Kids were in and out of our home all the time, and at camp, we would be packed out, and still had mother's at registration pleading with Debora and me to make room "just for their son"...It wasn't that we just lacked beds, but it was room in the dining room etc. Before long

Dave and Mary Ann Cox came to Brazil, and started the very first Word of Life Bible Institute. It grew and soon young people went forth starting WOL camps in other places. Today we have 6 WOL camps in six different States, and several Bible Institutes. WOL Bible clubs are progressing in many different cities and churches. We have much to praise and thank the Lord for. Being alone with the children for two weeks at a time, and two weeks with Dad in the house wasn't always easy. I had to tell Harry of the children's behavior, and that I had handled it...they didn't need discipline for the same wrong two times....God has been sooo good to our family. My mother's example and love of family surely paid off.

We were in Brazil a total of just under twenty years when God called us back to the US to direct the Overseas Program for WOL. Actually Harry and Harold often talked about the "success" of WOL in Brazil, and how this program could be used around the world. Really, what the guys did, was to pattern our work in Brazil after the pattern and example Jack Wyrtzen had set before them, and if we could do it in Brazil, others could do the same thing in other countries around the world.

The thrill for both Reimers and us was to see the number of young Brazilians, who left their lovely homes to serve the Lord in reaching the great Indian tribes of the North and central parts of Brazil...seemed like the work we had begun, the vision of the tribes of people, living in misery without the Lord, reached the heart of so many young Brazilians, and off they went to follow the Lord in those difficult places.

Returning to the USA was not a choice. The day came when Jack Wyrtzen told Harry he needed him to expand this ministry overseas. We'd tried other people in this leadership position, but all felt that it was on Harry's heart. He was the one to do it. So, we left, with many tears, departing from a country and people we had come to love. We felt like we belonged...we were not foreigners to them. Many expressed that if the Lord did not enlarge Harry's ministry they could not feel it was God's will for him to leave....Well, THAT was something to contend with. God knows what He is doing. The Overseas program took off, and soon there were missionaries opening WOL in Germany, Australia, the Philippines, Argentina, and on and on. Soon after our arrival in the US, Jack made Harry CO-director of the entire WOL ministry, and he gave Harry so much freedom in the ministry to do, and do as the Lord led him. Today there are WOL ministries on every continent of the world, in over 55 countries...with a goal, if God continues to lead, to have 100 WOL camps by 2010, or to be at least representing the Lord, in those countries by then.

How do I as wife and mother respond to all of this? Only, to God be the glory, and I just praise Him that He chose me to be Harry's wife over 58 years ago, that he gave me the health and desire to serve the Lord at his side. Namely, I was his wife, meeting his needs, raising our children in so many different places. Whatever ministry the Lord gave me with individuals, I only know that He has answered my prayer, because of remarks so many made, or wrote to me. When Harry and I were married, I was truly overwhelmed that he chose me to be his wife, and I remember praying, and asking the Lord to make our marriage an example to other young people who would also step out to serve Him anywhere. Thank you, Lord.

Now, if I didn't mention it, our four children all love the Lord as do their spouses, and all are serving the Lord. We have 11 grandchildren, all out of high school and profess to know the Lord. We are soon to be the proud great grandparents for the 2nd time...Our little great granddaughter, Lily Denae will soon be a big sister... and she is two years old. Three of our grandchildren are married to wonderful Christian guys. Has God blessed us? He really has.

# MY Story.....
## Gerda Hilda (Baumann) Kuykendall

I was born in Germany during the time that Adolf Hitler was in power. He made great promises to the people but the truth was the most of the Germans were destined for destruction along with the six million Jews. Hitler had a plan for a master race this meant the most of the German people would be disqualified. He was not going to let the people who had imperfection live. In 1940 he took 70,000 epileptic people and had them put to death because they were not perfect.

I was a very little girl when the war started. My father had to go off to war. We did not see him very much. Sometimes it would be a year between his visits. My uncles also had to go off to war.

At first the situation in Germany was not too bad. Hitler attacked other countries. And no one retaliated against Germany. So we lived pretty quiet. But when he started to attack England things changed for us. God had raised up a man for this time, Winston Churchill, who was not going to take it. He started, rightly so, to retaliate. That meant our country was turned upside down.

When the bombing raids started they came at night. That meant you could not sleep anymore. Even in the middle of winter, when it was freezing cold we had to get up and go into our cellar or to an air raid shelter. I cannot describe the fear that came over me. I did not know if I was going to live or not. Or if anything would be left when the air raid was over. You sit in the shelter hearing the bombs hit and the sound of buildings falling. The ground would shake like a major earthquake. Many of you have experienced earthquakes. Except this went on for an hour or more. When it was over with there was a sigh of relief. It was very very scary and not very pleasant.

On top of the fear you had the hunger. As the war progressed food and clothing started to become scarce. The stores had to close because food could not be transported or made. There just was nothing to sell. Sometime a store would get a shipment. They would put a sign in the window the time the store would be open. People would stand in line for hours to be first. We would get up in the middle of the night to be first in line because they would sell out very quickly. Some people would stand in line and get no food.

My mother had four little girls and could not leave us to go to stand in line. She would often send my sister Elisabeth and me to stand in line in the middle of the night. During the winter when the snow was on the ground it was very cold and we did not have any warm cloths. More than once the food ran out before we got any. We would get mad not because of not getting food but because we stood in line for nothing. Not thinking how our mother would feel not having food for her children. People got very inventive on how to find food. We had two palaces in our town. They had meadows and forest. It is amazing what you will eat when you are hungry. My sister and I would go there and eat berries and crawl around on the ground tasting different grasses and weeds trying to find ones we could eat. Some of them were edible. Later when I got to the United States and got into the victim mode I thought poor little old me I had to eat grass. Then one day I went into a health food store and found some of the grass we ate for sale at $5.95 a package.

My mother would go out into the country to beg for food. The problem was that many people were doing the same thing. Sometimes they would give her a piece of bread but not enough to feed her family. We lived in the city and had no way to have a garden. It was very hard for her having four little girls to feed and no husband to help.

My cousin Mariann was in her teen age years at this time. She would come to my house and say to my mother "Aunt Hilda can I take Gerda with me out into the country to beg for food'". She would let us go and we would be gone for one or two weeks at a time begging for food. The farmers would look down at little blue-eyed underweight little girl and feel sorry for me. We usually got a little something. When nighttime came we would be far from home so we would sleep in barns. This helped our moms tremendously because they did not have to feed us. Some times we would come home with a few potatoes and carrots or other vegetables that the farmers had given us.

Eventually there was no coal to cook with. My mother would take us little girls out to the woods and cut down little trees. My little sister and I were in charge of loading them onto a small wagon to haul home. It was a tremendous hardship for the ones with families to care for.

One day my mother got the news that her brother Ludwig had frozen to death on the Russian front. Sometime later she got the news that her other brother George was captured by the Czechoslovakian underground. His company had to dig a hole they knew that it was to be their grave and when they were done their life would be over, that they would be shot.

Both times when my mother received the news about her brothers she showed no emotion. My father away at war, her brothers' dead, the worries of caring for four little girls, destruction all around, finally she could not handle things anymore the proper way. Before I could come home and find a mother who was tender and caring all of a sudden that shut down because survival was priority number one. It took every thing out of her and she became cold and bitter toward every one and everything around because it was a fight just to stay alive and take care of your family.

She started to become very abusive physically and emotionally. Many times I would come home and find her in a bitter rage. She would slam me against the wall and tell me "You should never have been born" and "I wish you were dead". The punishment I feared the most was to be locked into the dark cellar. As a little child you can imagine all sorts of things were down there like mice and rats. I remember that on the top step there was a little crack at the bottom of the door that let a little ribbon of light in. I remember I could lay my head down on the step and peaking through the light and feeling good because at least there was some light. A lot of times it got dark because it was forgotten that I was in there. I did not want to bang on the door because that would bring more punishment. When there was no more light it was very very scary. I was always looking for light.

As a child it was easier because you do not have the responsibility to take care of family. And, you can go out and play and forget for a while. Only when things get real bad do the hunger, fears, agony and emotions come back.

Finally in 1945 the good news was that the war was over. We were so very happy. Just to go to bed and not be scared that you might survive during a bombing raid.

As little girls we dreamed that because the war was over it was going to be paradise and we will have food. We could eat chocolate and cake and have a lot of food. The sad reality was that for a long long time there was going to be much food. Life was still really devastating.

Every thing was in rubble, railways and roads were destroyed. Many of the men had died in the war or were still held in camps. Many on the Russian front that were missing never came back or came back many years later.

A few days after receiving the news that the war was over we were told that the Americans were coming in to our town and that we were to prepare to die. That they were going to come up the street and shoot every body. As children we did not know what to do with that information. How do you prepare to die?

We hung our white surrender sheets out of the windows. Then when the American soldiers marched up the street we all had to stand in front of our house. They went into each apartment or house to search for weapons or German soldiers. I remember that when they walked in we were trembling so much it was hard to stand still. They had been out in the field fighting for a long time and were dirty and tired. They looked very frightening to us little girls.

When they got ready to leave I told my sisters that they were not going to kill us now but probably would come back later. As they were leaving one of the soldiers, nodded toward us and smiled, I thought how mean can you get your going to kill somebody and here you are smiling. Thinking back he may have had a family at home too and was thinking of them, as he looked at us four little girls. He reached into his pocket and pulled something out and handed it to each of us little girls. It was something to eat. We thought oh my goodness they are not going to shoot us but are going to poison us instead. As hungry as we were I told my sisters not to eat it. It was hard to hold back because we were hungry. When we noticed he unwrapped it and put it in his mouth. When he did not fall over dead we thought all right we could go ahead and eat it. We unwrapped it put it in our mouths and started to chew. We chewed and chewed and noticed it did not disappear in our mouths. We thought what a wonderful little piece. What was it?...chewing gum! That was our first experience with chewing gum. When nighttime came and we should have thrown it away but we just could not part with it. We knew there was not going to be any more. Sooo…. we each found a safe place on the bed post to stick

The next morning we put it in our mouth and started to chew on it. And as you know it still has a little flavor left in it. But you know what happens after two weeks it gets black and hard as a rock. You have to say, "I must get rid of it or I will break my jaw".

The American people helped us out in a special way with our hunger. The call went out and your families donated to the Red Cross cloths and food. My mother was sent word to come to the Red Cross where she received a box containing milk powder, powdered eggs, dried potatoes and carrots that looked like french fries. We had no means to cook much so we would eat the potatoes and carrots uncooked. You could do it but it took a little time for them to get soft. But you know we were happy about it because we had something in our mouth for a long time.

We also got care packages from the United States. With clothes, shoes and blankets in them. The blankets we had my mother had taken and made coats out of them for us. It was cold and we really needed help.

When my mother got the first package and we were all very excited. She opened it and on top was a pair of football cleats on the top. My sister Elisabeth got the cleats. She would wear the to walk to school in. Because in the wintertime most of us just had rags wrapped around our feet to try and keep them warm and dry. She was happy to have the cleats. The only problem when I walked beside her to school I had to hear the clank - clank all the way there.

Some of you may have sent money or goods to the Red Cross or maybe your parents did. I would really like to take this opportunity to thank you from the bottom of my heart for being such a caring people and nation. We could not have made it with out your help.

I will never forget the kindness of the American Solider. At first they took our schools away for the troops to live in. As children we did not really mind not going to school. Pretty soon though they reopened them. They told us to bring our little lunch can and gave us soup and some bread to eat. They supplied us one meal a day. They also gave us physical examination and medicine.

Some of the soldiers used their own money and opened orphanages for the children whose parents were killed or missing. When I got to America and went to school for my citizenship I found out why the Americans were so different than the Russian Army. The Russians came into the east and destroyed, stole, ravaged the people and did nothing to help them get back on their feet. The Americans did everything to help us. I found the difference was that the Russians were atheist and had no respect for human life. America was founded on the principles of Christianity and because of that they respected life.

One day I came home and opened the kitchen door to find my father there. I will never forget how wonderful I felt to see him sitting at the kitchen table. He had been a prisoner of war in France.

He got a job as a janitor for the families of the American soldiers. The Americans took over some of the better German homes to house the dependent families. My father took care of about four of them.

Through this I was able to see how Americans lived. I thought it must be paradise. He would bring American magazines home and my sister and I would look through them in utter amazement. There would be a few pages of Max Factor make-up. On one page would be a woman with her face washed then we would turn the page and there she was with two or three things of make up dabbed on looking like a different person. It was amazing to us to see the hair color, nail polish and make up. We had never seen anyone with make up on like that.

One day my father came home with some hand-me-downs from the American children. We got just some little something nice to put on other than the black or gray clothes. There were little underwear with lace and socks with lace on the top and nice colorful dresses. This brought a little pleasure into our lives.

One day he came home with a pair of red paten leather shoes.

I was the oldest so I got to try them on first. I though when I set down to put them on that they were going to change my life. With those shoes I was going be Cinderella and live happily ever after. My dad had carved out two pieces of wood and nailed a leather strap on each and these were my shoes. I sat down and pulled those ugly things off my skinny little legs to slip in to those red paten leather shoes. The problem was I had a hard time getting my foot in because they were one size to small. As you know when there are a pair of shoes you really must have you can manage to get them on. I finally squeezed them on and stood up to walk into the sunset into my happy new life. The problem was that when I started walking there was an agonizing pain shooting from my big toe up to my brain saying you cannot continue walking with that pain. So I finally set down and my life fell apart as I pulled those beautiful shoes off.

Then I hear the football cleat girl coming by the window. She comes in and guess what? Her feet slipped smoothly into those shoes. I was unhappy for a long time. And I really did not like her very much. But life did go on and now we are not only sisters but also best friends.

Because I was so amazed about America I wanted to find a way to get there. I read magazines about German singers and dancers when they became famous would be invited to America to perform and then stay there. I had my dream to become a singer and dancer never thinking that I did not have the talent. I remember going to ballet class and seeing all these girls who were very bendable. Here I was stiff as a board and very unbendable. Singing with others my voice was just O.K. So that dream also died. I thought "Alright I will never make it to the U. S".

Thankfully God knew things that I did not. He knew that when I was a tiny little girl I was not going to die in the war. He had one young man in America for me. He got tired of people telling him what to do, when to go to bed when to get up, what to wear and how to cut his hair, so he joined the Army. He woke up really quick.

God arrange it for him to be sent far far from home to Germany where he was very lonely.

One of his buddies was dating a German girl and they invited him to her mother's house for dinner one Saturday. They were cooking on propane and they ran out of gas. God was in control even of that. They came over to my mom's house to see if they could finish cooking there.

It was Saturday and that was cleaning day for us. I had on an old pair of baggy pants with a rope for a belt, my hair in a pig tail when they came in. I weighed 89 lbs.. I was in a corner on my hands and knees scrubbing the floor. The first time he saw me he thought I was a 12 year old girl, I was 17. Here was this handsome young man in uniform and he did not even look at me. So while they went back to get the food I got busy.

I had worked as a housekeeper for American families and would dig out the make up they threw away. So I dabbed some on, brushed out my hair, put on my one and only nice dress. When they came back I did notice he was paying attention.

I sat at the table next to him and buttered his bread. That was all it took. We were going to get married I was his Cinderella and he was my prince charming and we would live happily ever after.

He told me he was taking me to the most wonderful place in the world. We arrived in New York after an 8 day trip on a troop ship. I was sea sick the entire trip. Then flew to his paradise. It was June 6th and the doors of the plane opened. The air hit me it was 100 degrees, 100 percent humidity, we were in Texas. This was not paradise to me.

After about three months we moved to California. There were no jobs where he lived in Texas. His sister in California invited us there and they would help us get settled. By this time we had two little children.

John found a job and after a few weeks we had our own place and were pretty much alone. I was removed from everything that had been familiar to me. I was away from my family. I was totally overwhelmed. Just going to the market was a fearful thing. There on the shelves were 10 kinds of bread to choose from, 5 different kinds of green bean and so on. In Germany we went to a little corner market where we had few if any choices. John had to take me home the first time I went shopping because I could not handle it. I'm O.K. now with my double coupons and sales papers.

I was very introverted and fearful of people because during the war you could not trust your neighbor or even you friend. If you said something politically incorrect you could be arrested and sent to a camp. I became very home sick and there was nothing I could do about it.

Here I was, all alone with my own little family and I found myself doing to them all the things I had hated that was done to me.

Every thing in Germany was a regimented life. People only counted if they could produce something for the masses. The country had to be kept in order. You were raised not to cry because that would bring shame on you and be a sign of weakness. I was raised with no feelings and could not express myself. Every thing around me and in me was dark and ugly.

Where I lived we had separate boys and girls schools. Even when we went to school we could not go out and just play. During recess we would go outside and walk around in a circle. If you stepped out of line there was someone there to punish you.

This happened to my friend and I. We were taken to the office where the teacher made us straiten out our hands and she struck us several time with a stick in the open palm. But the worse thing was she bent over me and said to me "you should have never been born and you will never amount to anything and you are no good".

What happens on the inside is a strong dislike of self and depression sets in. When you are like that you cannot be nice and loving. That is not good family material.

Here I was with my own sweet children but not seeing them as individuals. I wanted to keep the house in order and often they were in the way. I got ugly to them. This broke my heart so I thought if I am going to hurt somebody I would be better if I were dead. So I took a razor blade to cut my wrist. Fortunately when a little blood appeared I got scared and stopped. That would not have been an answer at all.

My husband found out that he had not married Cinderella. But he was a man who had made a commitment before God, until death do us part. He was going to stay with us no matter what. It was hard for him and he knew he needed some help. He was a Christian but had not been going to church for a while. He decided he needed to get back to church and let God help him. He started going to church with the children but I told him I was not going. I had been brought up religious. I was taken to church when I was a baby and a religious ceremony took place and it was pronounced that from then on I was a Christian and was going to heaven. I had religious instruction in school by government religious teachers who never used the bible. I had to go to church in order to get a good grade on my report card. The god they talked about was a god of fear.

When air raids came and we were in school we went to the shelters. It was full of little scared children. When we cried we were told "God is watching if you do not stop God will punish you". My religion was full of fear and a God that was not very nice and not someone I wanted to be close to.

After a while my conscience got the best of me as I watched my children and husband go to Church. I decided to go with them. To my amazement the pastor read out of the Bible and talked about a different God than I had heard of.

What was amazing to me was when the pastor read out of Psalm 139 about how God is always there and that we cannot go any where that he is not with us.

How he is holding our hand and has one hand laid upon us.

People had told me many times that I was worthless and should never have been born. Then he read 139:13-18 about how God had formed me and that I was fearfully and wonderfully made, how He put me in my mother's womb. That He had written in a book the day I would be born and when I would die.

I did not believe it when he read those words I thought he was lying. I decided to go home and get the Bible out and read it for myself. Sure enough that is what it said. Can you imagine what good news that was to me? All of a sudden I was somebody. I thought that God was nice after all.

God still had to teach me that He was more than able to help me. I was still looking inside of me. My countenance never changed. People thought I was like a solid rock. But inside I was emotionally disturbed and longing for help. I wanted to be happy I wanted to be loving and gentle and kind. I saw people around me that were like that. I felt I was trapped and there was no way out of my plight. I prayed "God please help me". That is all I knew to do.

Then I read in the Bible in Exodus how God led the people of Israel out of Egypt. When Pharaoh finally had let them go from slavery he then changed his mind and started chasing after them to bring them back. They came to the Red Sea and had no way to cross. Here they were trapped and no way out. God moved a cloud behind them to hide them. Then as they slept he parted the sea and made a way for them to escape. Like it says in Psalm 121:3,4 God never sleeps. While they were sleeping God was working to help them. Even when I did not know it God was working for me. And He is doing same for you.

I thought my problems were too big for God. Then I realized that parting the Red Sea was a miracle. I did not even know God could do miracles. Then hope came to me when I realized that that sea was a whole lot bigger and wilder than me and if He could part a big sea then He could help a little person like me.

But nothing was happening because God still had to teach me more. He first wanted me to be His child. I thought I was because of the religious ceremony that was performed over me as a baby.

Then I heard that Jesus said, "I am the way and the truth and the life and no one comes to the Father but through me". This got me to thinking that there was something about being a child of God that I did not understand.

Then I read John 3:16 "For God so loved the world that He gave His only begotten Son that who ever believes in Him should not perish but have eternal life". Finally I understood, slowly but surely, that no one could make me a Christian that it was my own personal decision to ask Jesus to come into my life. Like it says in Romans 10:10 "For with the heart a person believes, resulting in righteousness and with the mouth he confesses resulting in salvation."

Before when I went to church it was all about following rules and regulation, but this time something had happened inside of me. My heart was totally involved and there was this longing to be a child of God. I went on my knees and ask Jesus to come in and to be my Lord and Savior. What a wonder that was because in me there had been no peace, nothing but deep dark blackness and fear. All of a sudden when Jesus came in there was peace and there was light and hope. It was really marvelous thing to be born again.

The Bible says that when you are born again something supernatural happens inside. The Holy Spirit came in and I became a new creation (2nd. Corinthians 5:17).

> He turned my fear to peace,
> My despair and coldness to love,
> He healed all my emotional pain.
> For the first time in my life there was peace and
>    light in my inner being.

God can change a life Isaiah 41:10 God said to me "I will help you I will strengthen you- I will lift you up with my victorious right hand."

There was I lot of work for God to change in my life. I found out that for Him to change me I had to start reading the Bible and talking to Him. As I read the Bible and talked to Him my heart begin to soften. When I did get upset I would go to the Bible and there would be a verse like "Don't be afraid.....

Day by day slowly but surely God changed my life.

Then He made me aware that I had to go to my mother. My unforgiveness of her was an ugly heavy weight inside of me that made me bitter. God brought things to my mind about my mother. Like do you remember when there was no food and she went begging for you. Or remember how she would go out in the day time and find some field with food growing and then in the night go back and steal it. The fields were heavily guarded and anyone found stealing would be shot right there no questions asked

One night she came home with frozen fingers from digging in the cold ground.. I saw her open those frozen fingers and about 8 or 10 brussel sprouts on to the table. God showed me that this is the way she showed her love. Not the way I thought it should be loved, but in the only way she could show it.

I looked into her background and found out that she was the oldest of six children. Her mother was always sick and she was expected to take care of the other children. There was never any tenderness shown to her. No one to say "I love your". These things are learned. And if you have no one around you to show you then the only one who can teach you is God.

She finally had to leave home very young because of abuse. Then there was the guilt of leaving the other brothers and sisters. She got married very young. Soon after marriage my father went to the army. Then the war and all the tragedy and suffering war brings. Then having four little girls to protect and care for.

It was very easy the way God led me to forgive her. I was able to put my arms around her and say "I love your" but she was never able to respond. But you could tell that she really appreciated that someone really cared for her.

My next lesson was that God wanted to teach me was to say "I am sorry". I had never said to my husband that I was sorry for something. My husband did something to make me really mad and I responded in a not so nice way. Even though I thought I had a right to be mad. God said I had to say "I am sorry to him". I really thought God had not said that to me. But there was no peace and God would not let me go on. He was laying on the couch in the family room. I started in the back of the house ran by him and on the way by quickly said "sorry" I continued on down the hall and around the corner. He though he had heard wrong, sat up and said "what did you say. I said "God please help him understand what I said" because I cannot do it again. God answered my prayer. It was quite a struggle but now I find it easy. I really pray that I will not do wrong in the first place.

I was able to go to each of my Children and ask forgiveness. The miracle was that they do not remember much about those times. God had done another miracle for me by helping them forget.

God is the only one who could take a stubborn German like me and turn me around. I could not do it by myself. He is still working with me I am not finished yet.

I am now able to look back at all of my life and see the truth of Romans 8:28, 29 . "And we know that God causes all things (Even the bad things) to work together for good to those who love God, to those who are called according to *His* purpose. For those whom He foreknew, He also predestined *to become* conformed to the image of His Son, so that He would be the firstborn among many brethren;...."

# MY Story...Judy Shoff
# NO REGRETS

I was born into what I always thought was just an average family. However, the longer I live the more I have come to realize that my family was truly extraordinary.

We did not have much money, yet one of my earliest memories was living in a one bedroom apartment connected to a basement church where my Dad was the custodian. My parents just come through the Great Depression and our possessions were meager, but I never thought of us as being poor.

One of the lasting memories I have of my early childhood, was the empty glass quart milk bottle that always sat in the center of our kitchen table. My parents would put all their loose change at the end of each day. This money was to go toward the project that they had undertaken – to buy an automobile for a missionary family that was serving in a rural area in the deep South.

It was a joyous day when as a five year old I was allowed to go with my parents to purchase that automobile. My parents didn't own a car at the time, but how thrilled and excited we were to present the car to this family when they came "North" to receive their gift.

Prayer was a very significant part of daily life, for my parents. Each day – sometimes in the morning after breakfast and sometimes in the evening I recall kneeling at a wooden chair in that little kitchen with my Mom on one side and Dad on the other as we "talked to Jesus."

Ours was a spiritual home. It seemed that life centered around the Bible. Whether we were at church or at home.

Mom held "Good News Clubs" with a simple flannel graph board, inviting the kids in our neighborhood in for punch and cookies and teaching them the stories of the Bible.

When I was a young teen we moved from Illinois to California, and immediately sought out a "good" church in which to be involved.

Mom began her club again, only this time it was "Kings Kids" a simple study of God's Word and some games, and of course, punch and cookies.

During those teenage years, I loved to read. Any book in the school library was just fine, and through my reading, I began to formulate a plan for my future.

Even though I was in a lot of ways very shy, I looked forward to the time when I would be all grown up and not be under my parents' strict authority. Their were rules like, no makeup, no movies, no dances, no staying out late, no going out alone with a boy, and on it went.

In my immature mind, I began to think that my parents were keeping me from having the "fun" in life that all the other teenagers seemed to be having.

I was about 15 when my brother, two years younger that I decided that he wanted to join the "church", and great discussion took place around our dinning room table about this decision.

It was decided that "yes, he would join the church" and the next Sunday morning when the pastor gave his closing invitation my brother would go forward and declare that he wanted to join the church.

Then, there in the dinning room, it became very silent and it seemed that both my parents were staring at me as if, since I, the older sister, should also "join the church."

So, because I did not want to cause commotion or reveal the rebellion in my heart against the "Christian way", I too, went forward to "join the church."

The pastor shook our hands, and told us to come that evening to be baptized.

So we did, just that. I went down a dry rebellious teen and came out of those waters a wet rebellious teen. And that was it.

Graduating from high school early, I had a difficult time adjusting to a new way of life as a college student, and after one semester at a junior college, my parents decided to send me to a Christian college, clear across the country because they happened to know the Dean of Men and his wife.

In my heart I thought, - finally, I have a chance to get away from my "Christian" parents and maybe, just maybe, I can have a chance to have the fun and fulfillment in life that I was looking for.

Wow, was I wrong. The rules were strict and under classman were not allowed to go off campus without a chaperone. Yet, in spite of the "rules", I was enjoying the social life and getting attention from the young men on campus.

Although dating was restricted to the special event on the campus or in the "dating parlor" which was chaperoned by the professors, I was having a great time…..until one night I received a "note" under the door of my room from a young man. Of course, my roommates were excited, and so was I but I had no idea who he was. So out came one of last year's annuals and my roommates discovered that the young man was an important upperclassman, president of a student organization and leader on campus. Everyone was excited.

Well, after one date with this handsome young man I determined he definitely was not for me. All he talked about was the off-campus weekend ministry he was involved in and the summer Youth Revivals he and his buddy would be leading. His life goal was to be a "preacher". That was definitely not in my book. A preacher's wife - how dull. No way did I want another date with a young man who was so overpoweringly "religious".

The young man was quite persistent, regularly asking for dates, and getting turned down continually. Summer vacation came, and my mom was determined to send me back to that same school in the Fall.

Much to my dismay, back for the fall semester, I found my assigned seat in chapel and there was that handsome "preacher boy" seated in the row right in front of me. It was disgusting. But the seats were assigned and I had no out, but to try to smile and reject his requests for a date.

Several months into the semester, my roommates invited me to come to a movie with them. I was excited thinking we would be able to go off campus to a real theatre, since one of the roomies was a senior. But it was not to happen that way. Instead, I found myself in the campus auditorium watching a movie about a young man who had dedicated his life to God and became a missionary to Africa!

Oh, I was upset, almost angry, walking back to the dorm that night. In the middle the campus we came upon the crosswalk. One way led to our dorm, the other to the auditorium, another to the dinning room, etc.

As we made the turn at that crosswalk, something happened in my heart. I felt like I was getting a direct message from above. "This crosswalk represents a decision, and tonight is your night of decision. You can continue to go in your rebellious way or you can make a choice to accept and follow me, Jesus. It's your choice." My heart was pounding.

After "lights out" I lay in my top bunk of the dorm room and it seemed as though I was wrestling with God. I my mind He was letting me see the people I idolized, and the disastrous lives to which they had succumbed. I wanted "the world" and the fun, but sometime in the middle of the night tossing in that bunk, I turned me face into my pillow and talked with the Lord. I knew I had a rebellious spirit within me, though for the most part it had been kept well hidden. I knew I was a sinner, though I had not outwardly committed any gross sins. I knew that Jesus came to offer me the gift of salvation, and finally after what seemed an eternity of wrestling I prayed and asked the Lord Jesus to come into my life, forgive me of my sins and make me the person He wanted me to be. And I fell soundly asleep.

The next morning, as I was preparing for the day, I felt such peace. Brushing my hair in front of the mirror, I whispered another prayer. This time it went something like - " Dear Lord, I really meant what I said last night, and to show you I mean it, I will even be willing go to - (the most repulsive thing I could think of) yes, Lord, I will even go to Africa for you, amen.." Then, as an after thought, I whispered, "and Lord Jesus, I will even give you my date life."

That was it.

Well, two days later on Monday morning, chapel was starting and in walks the handsome preacher boy, smiling, and asking, as usual, "How's little Judy, today?"

The very same question he had asked over and over again during the past weeks, but this time instead of a hostile reaction, little Judy simply replied, "Fine, she's just fine."

And that was the beginning of the greatest, most beautiful chaperoned courtship and church wedding. We set out for seminary so that my new husband could finish his seminary education and prepare for a life of ministry. Sure, we have had our tough times and times when I felt like I couldn't see any light at the end of the dark tunnel. Yes, we were very young and probably pretty naïve, but one thing I learned from my new husband, was that he believed the Bible literally and endeavored to put it into practice in every area of our lives.

He was in seminary, working part time in a meat market, I was working in a savings and loan, and we were living in a basement apartment. Money was so tight. Between the two of us we averaged about $85 a week. $88 a month for rent, a car payment, groceries and seminary tuition took every cent, BUT the "tithe", God's part, always came first. I tried to reason with my man, but his answer was "Honey, if we can't trust God to take care of us now, we have no business in the ministry." That has been a motto of our lives, as we watched the Lord, miraculously over the past 50 years supply our every need, and over and above all that we could have ever asked or thought. His way is true.

There in that little basement apartment, one morning after Don left for school, I set up all the bills across the back of the little sofa, and knelt down before them and prayed. "Dear Lord, we have been faithful and obedient to you, now what am I supposed to do about these bills?"

Arriving at the Savings and Loan, getting ready for the day's work I set down at my desk, and there propped on the desk was a legal size envelope with my name on it. Hesitantly, I opened it to find a $20 bill. No note, no nothing! My first thought was, this must be some kind of test that the management puts new employees through. I'll just leave it on the desk until I can talk to a manager...but before that happened; later in the morning one of the secretaries (who was also a

Believer) and I were speaking together. I told her about the envelope and she replied, "I put it there, it's for you. I have been putting aside extra money in my top drawer and for the last few days it was as if God was telling me to give it to you. I don't know why, but it is a gift from me to you via Jesus."

She didn't know our desperate needs, and in those days $20 was a lot of money. This was my first big lesson in learning to trust the Lord in all things.

While Don was in seminary he was asked to go speak to a small group of people meeting in a cement block building on the North edge of town, who wanted to start a church in their area. Churches were scarce in that part of town. The few people that were meeting together there, were very accepting of us as a young family, and so together we worked and prayed and begin to build a body of believers worshipping together on Sunday mornings and evenings. Eventually we moved to a larger barrack building next to a railroad track. On Sunday mornings when the train came through and the whistle blew, the sermon had to stop until that dear engineer passed by and we could hear again. (In those days there were no sound systems to drown out peripheral noises.) In spite of all the inconveniences, people kept coming to the Lord. Soon we realized we needed more space for a children's program and better facilities during the cold winter months.

Then the opportunity came for the congregation to purchase half a city block (near the edge of town in a better neighborhood, which was a tremendous opportunity and seemingly an answer to our prayers. Yet we were faced with an impossibility. These were working class people who lived week-to-week and there was no way they could raise the funds to purchase the land. But they did.

When the property was secured, we took another giant step of faith. Don was still in seminary. He decided to give up his small salary from the church and go back to working nights, cutting meat in the freezer room of the local super market. Just a few hours of sleep and lots of coffee and off he went to class at the seminary

The building began to take shape and before long we moved into what was, for that little congregation, not only a beautiful building, but also a monument of a miracle. The church continued to grow and many men and women came to faith in Christ. Those were exciting days, as we saw rough rodeo men and wayward women come to the Lord and have their lives transformed. People had to stand at the back of the building because there was no room to sit.

One of the men known in the area for chasing off every "preacher" that ever came near his home came to the Lord and was baptized. It was the talk of that community. People came just to see "Old Buck" in church.

The Lord kept blessing, yet I had the longing to be closer to my parents. During one particularly lonely time, I knelt down at our little sofa and committed our lives afresh to the Lord. "I'll stay here Lord, but you will have to take the fear of tornados from me and help me not to miss my family at holidays." (That was shortly before Don's graduation from seminary.)

Four months later, we received a call from a group of people in our denomination to come to California to help start a church. There were about 50 people meeting in a wedding chapel, in a very fast growing area of the state.

So, with a U Haul trailer behind us, we along with our two children, made our way to a new venture – starting a church in California. And the people came and came, and, again we were finding property and putting up a church building.

During those days of busyness I found myself struggling in my inner self. Since the church was growing quickly and Don was in the limelight a lot, I desperately wanted to be the perfect pastor's wife. I worked hard to keep my house perfect, worked desperately to look the part of a perfect preacher's wife, nagged my husband, and children to be more perfect, and kept up a pretty good front. I went back to college to get my degree in Education while the girls were in school. I taught Sunday School, and delivered Avon in the neighborhood for a little extra spending money.

While all this was going on I was also making weekly trips to the Doctor's office. I couldn't sleep. I was tired all day. I had headaches, stomach pains and tightness in my chest. I was taking pills to keep me awake, pills to help me sleep, pills to give me energy and pills to help me relax. At one point the doctor said to me, "You are going to have to get a hold on yourself or your husband will have to leave the ministry." So I went home, and worked a little harder to be perfect, and prayed that the Lord would help me to do a better job at everything.

It seemed that my husband was so busy building a church he didn't realize that I had some deep needs. I resented the church. I wanted his attention. There were days when I was so despondent that I would think about driving my car into the ocean and ending everything. Then I would be a peace in heaven. But then I would think about my young family, and would turn around and head for home.

We were invited to a special conference, held in a very fancy hotel. I was thrilled to get away, and be somewhere where a lot of big names in the Christian community would be. It was a big time for me.

The conference offered many different workshops. We decided that we would each go to a different session and bring back the information gleaned. We would cover twice as much ground that way. It sounded great. So off I went to my seminar, perfectly groomed, notebook and Bible in hand.

When I arrived at the meeting room, it was packed -- standing room only. An usher was turning people away at the door, but did offer to tell those at the door that there was some space up front for anyone who would like to sit on the floor. I was enraged. How dare he think "I" would lower myself and sit on the floor in ANY conference. After all, I was the pastor's wife. And I turned away in a huff.

But then something within me made stop and think. If this seminar is packed – it must be pretty good. Maybe I had better stay."

So I turned around and made my way over books and feet to find a space up near the front – on the floor. The speaker had already begun his talk. He was telling the story of his own life. Although he was a minister and Editor-in-chief of <u>Decision Magazine</u>, he told of his cruel tongue, cutting people at the office and even his own wife, down to size.

He told about being called up to do a story on the revival that was going on in Canada. The caller remarked "We're walking knee-deep in love up here."

As he went on telling us about his experience with the Lord in an After Glow service up there, I began to cry. I didn't know why, I just couldn't stop crying. I couldn't take notes. In fact, my notebook paper was covered with tears, and by the end of his session I was an absolute mess.

At the conclusion of his seminar there were a number of people around him waiting to talk to him. When I finally was able to speak with him, all I could say was, "I need what you were talking about today."

He didn't pat me on the back and say, "Poor thing, let's pray." He didn't sympathize with me. It was just a curt "Go backstage over there behind the stage curtain, kneel down at a chair and pray."

So I did as he said and prayed as hard as I knew how. It went something like this: "Dear Lord, you know how hard I work for you in the church, in my home, and on my marriage. I try so hard to be perfect. You know how hard I try to be kind, etc, etc."

Well, it was a long wait, I began to wonder if anyone was ever going to come and rescue me from that chair. Finally, Dr. Sherwood Wirt, the speaker came over. He didn't ask my name, he didn't ask my problem. He just said, very non- emotionally, "Tell God who you are bitter toward."

My internal reaction was: "How dare you think 'I' have bitterness in my heart toward anyone. After all, 'I' am a preacher's wife; 'I' am trying so hard to be perfect. 'I', 'I', 'I'-. But he quietly answered my silence by repeating the same statement, "Tell God who you are bitter toward."

More silence and a third time the same statement. I began to think in my heart, this guy is not going to let me get up from this chair until I say something. And then slowly, I began to think maybe I did have bitterness in my heart, and slowly the words began to come out,"Mrs. So and so, because she didn't…..; Mr. So and so, because he did…; and John Doe because he wasn't…… ." On I went, and then, from the pit of my stomach came the wrenching word against my own dear husband, because he wasn't meeting my needs, and he surely did not understand how hard 'I' was trying to be a good wife.

My heart and my real self were laid open before this important minister. He had no reaction, no sympathy. His next statement was simply, "Now ask God to crucify you." That was all he said. And he waited silently.

Again my mind reacted and I silently thought, "How dare you say that!" I'm a Christian, I have accepted Jesus Christ as my Savior, AND 'I'm" a pastor's wife!

But he repeated the same simple statement, and again in the silence of the moment I had no verbal response. "Hey, don't you know who 'I' am!!" I thought, but after the third time he made that statement, I begin to realize what he was saying. He was asking me to ask the Lord to crucify "ME". The almighty "I" that I was so enamored with. The ME that all my concerns revolved around - ME!

Slowly I began to realize that the ego in me needed to die, to be nailed to the cross and be crucified, and get out of the way so Jesus Christ could begin to work through this shell of a woman.

And even more slowly now, I croaked out the words, "Dear Lord, I ask you in Jesus name to crucify ME." That was all.

Dr. Wirt helped me to my feet, and simply said, "You won't feel any different, but wait a few weeks and see what happens."

I got up and tried to pat my face so I wouldn't look like I had been crying, and walked out the door to find my husband anxiously waiting for me.

I simply said to him, "Please don't ask me what happened in there today. Maybe someday I'll be able to tell you, but not now." And wise man that he is, he didn't ask.

Well, that was the beginning of a new life for me. Nothing happened, really. Until one day, several weeks later, someone from the church came by to visit, and remarked, "Judy, I've been watching you lately. I thought it was a new show you were putting on, but it seems that you are different and that you really love the people at the church. You just seem different."

I begin to reflect. Yes I was different. I no longer had the headaches, I wasn't taking the pills that I had needed so desperately to get through a day, and most of all the horrible pain in the pit of my stomach was gone, and I often found myself humming praise songs during the day. I was different!

It was a new life. Oh, sure there are always the ups and downs, but life took on new purpose. It seemed that I was no longer consumed with "ME". I began to find real joy in serving others wherever it might be. It was exciting to watch other people grown and mature in the Lord, and our home life, seemed to me, to be so much more peaceful. Music filled the air.

In the church, I found myself organizing a Women's' Ministry, and to my own amazement began teaching a Sunday morning Women's Bible Class and I found a great sense of fulfillment having people over for meals at our home.

I believe, with all my heart, that if the Lord hadn't gotten hold of me that day under the guidance of Dr. Wirt, our marriage would probably have ended, I would have alienated my children, and probably wouldn't even be alive today.

Since then we have had opportunities to travel and minister to people in a number of countries.

We led several trips to Israel, and on one of those trips, spent several days touring Egypt. Our guide directed us to his cousin who sold "good" water. And trusting his judgment we bought some of his bottled water. It's a good thing we were going home, because I became deathly sick from the water. Shortly after arriving home from this trip we received a call from one of our church missionaries. "Guess what," she said excitedly. "You're going to Africa!"

I thought, "No, no, no, not me. I am sick as a dog just from being in Egypt, I can't go to Africa."

But several months later we were headed to Zimbabwe to speak at a mission conference. Then to Nigeria, to visit another of our missionaries, on to Tanzania and Kenya.

Traveling in Africa with AIM International, at one of the mission stations, I watched a baby die in its mother's arms as she sat despondently in the yard of the mission dispensary after the nurse there did all she could. We tried to comfort her with a loving hug around her shoulders, unable to communicate verbally.

Landing at another mud airfield, we carefully made our way on a felled tree trunk across a deep ravine, to have a meal in the round, mud hut of a couple who had accepted the Lord in that territory. They graciously carried a basin of water around as we sat on their cots, to wash our hands before we ate from the pot of something cooking in the middle of the hut on an open fire.

I prayed, "Dear Lord, I will put it in my mouth, please help me keep it down" and He answered that prayer that day, and other times as we visited remote villages. The people are so gracious. Their needs are so few. Some nights I would lay awake thinking, what would these people do if they saw a super market stocked so full of every item imaginable. They had never even seen a store! Yet they were happy.

Wherever we went the children would rush out to the air field as our single engine airplane would land. They wanted to touch "the pealed ones" referring to our skin so white in sharp contrast to their own.

Everywhere, everywhere, a smile and a loving touch brought connection, and the sense of being worthwhile was overwhelming.

After arriving back home in the states, in the quietness of our bedroom, my husband would often verbalized to me that he dreamed of ministering to missionaries on the field. I thought he was having nightmares, and would always dismiss the thought. Then out of the blue the call came to ask us to serve with a mission. He was thrilled. I was not. We had a vital ministry going on in Southern California, a healthy, growing church and all the comforts of our "community" and a lifestyle we were enjoying. I loved our ministry and all the connections we had formed.

Yet in spite of my tears, and pleading, in the depths of my heart, I believed this was something we had to do, even though I didn't want to. In the airplane, on our way home to the West Coast after being interviewed by the mission board, I cried hysterically, "Can't you change your mind, can't you change your mind."

Looking back on that episode, I wonder if the attendants and nearby passengers thought we were going through a divorce.

And so, we left our comfortable ministry and moved to the East Coast to be involved with a foreign mission society for a period of time.

I was lonely, out of my comfort zone, involved in the office during most days, and traveling with my husband on weekends, as he spoke in mission conferences. It was a difficult time for me. But it was a rich experience in my life to find new, wonderful, lasting friendships and the encouragement I needed during that time. I was being stretched to trust the Lord in new circumstances.

Traveling again through Africa to visit mission stations represented by the agency, we had just arrived at the "Guest House" in Nairobi, after being in "the bush" for a period of time. There was a phone call and I was called to the phone to hear my Dad at the other end of the line, asking for us to come home as quickly as possible, as my Mom was not expected to live. We made arrangements, and able to secure passage back to the States three days later. On the trip home, Don came down with high fever, and, we found out later he was suffering from malaria. Somehow the medication for malaria did not afford him the protection he needed.

We arrived home three days before my Mom went home to Glory, and Don did the funeral with 103 degree temperature, still sick from the malaria.

Soon, we realized we missed the pastorate, and needed to be back in church ministry. That was when a small church in the greater Los Angeles area, we had visited, called to ask if we would consider their need for a minister.

After two trips back to California the church called us, and soon we found ourselves getting settled in the beautiful foothills of Southern California.

Another exciting adventure was about to unfold.

We were excited about being able to work with this small congregation which had been without a pastor for two years.

The first 18 months of ministry there were, to say the least, discouraging. It seemed nothing was getting accomplished. The church wasn't growing, the budget wasn't being met and we were discouraged. After one particularly discouraging Sunday evening, my husband and I pulled into the garage and just sat there and talked. It wasn't an easy time. We thought that our time of ministry was over, but that night my husband made some serious decisions with the Lord and a new commitment to ministry. (You can read about it in Leadership Magazine, Spring 1996, entitled, <u>Die Climbing, a Testimony of</u> <u>Renewal</u>).

It was about that time that several families decided to leave the church to start their own ministry. I was certain that I would have to go back to teaching school in order for us to survive financially. But much to our surprise, the very next Sunday the budget was met, people started coming and the congregation began to grow.

Before long we had other problems, where to put the people. It was decided to begin a second worship service, and then necessity demanded a third service, and later even a Saturday evening worship.

It was evident that the Lord was blessing and bringing people to this congregation. I loved having a part in establishing a Women's Ministry Board and teaching women's Bible Studies, developing a Sunday morning class for college students, establishing "Rebuilders" – a class for single, and single again adults, and, later CASA a, career and single adult ministry.

The work became overwhelming and we were now past the traditional time for retirement. The desire to retire from pastoring a church was on my husband's heart. I worried. How would we live? Would our Social Security pension cover our needs? Could we keep up our home? Wouldn't we get bored not having a "church" to serve? These were nagging questions on my heart, but in spite of the fear of the unknown for me....he retired.

For our retirement the church had a "This is your life" party with people from our former churches, as well as family and missionary friends come to be a part of the program. That was a total surprise to us. How blessed we were, looking out over the huge group of attendees to think that here were people who had made an impact on our lives coming to wish us well.

Retired? What is that? I had a list of "honey-dos," that has been growing over the years. I thought that finally some of these projects would be accomplished.

Now that was a joke!!!

Don had a passion for ministering to pastors in the smaller churches in our area.

He began to seek out the men in ministry and formed accountability groups that meet together for guidance, accountability and encouragement.

Along with this work, he began to associate with Titus Ministries, working with churches that have gone through difficult circumstances; need counsel in organization, team building or outreach, and interim pastoring when necessary.  Our first assignment became a two-year project working with a church about an hour from us. I couldn't imagine how we could keep up such a pace, and identify with people in a totally different area than we were used to.

But, again, the Lord was leading and we found it so rewarding to get to know these beautiful people and work with them in serving the Lord.  After two years, the church was able to call a new pastor, and we "passed the baton".  We had established some very dear and lasting friendships there which have truly blessed our lives.

After that assignment, Titus sent us to work with a church in Illinois!!!  We became part of the "jet set" flying back and forth to lead this congregation through a transition period.  And again, even though it was only for four months, the people were wonderful and we have formed some more wonderful friendships.

Our two daughters have blessed us with their wonderful husbands, and 5 terrific grandchildren.  For the past several years we have had what we call "Cousins Camp" for our daughters and their families.

It has become of time when we go to a resort or beach house, and just hang together.  We do crafts, have Bible stories and make special meals, but the highlight for our grandchildren has become "Grandpa's Treasure Hunt".

The project involves my husband seeking out hiding places, and writing out the clues. I love watching him walk through the house and grounds when the kids are busy somewhere else, trying to conjure up his hiding places and clues to go along with them. There is always a special treat in the treasure chest.

Looking back, over my life, so overwhelmingly full of family, ministry and friendships, I can truly say, that my life message is:

> Live according to the principles in the Book of Life.
> Obey those principles even when you don't want to
> Keep your eyes on Jesus.
> Offer a smile and a gently touch to everyone,
> ...and you will find a life of purpose and peace, and NO REGRETS.

# MY STORY.....LILLIE KNAULS

Church was the first place I went in life. I grew up in a Christian home and each time the church door opened the Knauls family walked through. Six girls and one boy. I don't remember not loving the Lord and knowing that, I received Jesus at a young age. I also know that life would have been very different without this decision.

An Arkansas native, I was born the fifth of seven children. In l951, my father passed away. The family then moved to Seattle, Washington where I continued my education through high school, graduating in 1965. Suffering from mild dyslexia, I opted for a career at the Pacific Phone Company rather than pursuing a college degree. I recently attended my 50th high school class reunion, where I was honored to be asked to sing two songs.

In 1963 I became engaged to be married but broke the engagement just months prior to the wedding. I began to feel the relationship was not God's will. Soon dating began again, but eventually I realized that marriage was not in God's plan for my life. I asked God to please give me my husband if it was His will for me to be married, and if He wanted me to be single I asked Him to give me the gift of singleness. As time went by, I felt it was God's plan for me to have a season of singleness.

To this day I remain a happy single woman, but must confess that for a period of time I struggled with the idea of living single. One of the main challenges of living the single life was the difficulty of letting my life be a witness for God while coping with my human emotions such as loneliness, frustration and anxiety. However, this has been conquered. I am single and satisfied. In

1st Corinthians 7, the Lord offers happiness to some with the gift of being single and to others the gift of being married.

I was taught by my Mom that God loved me and had a plan for my life. My desire was to stay close to Him so that I could hear His direction. After breaking my wedding engagement I transferred my job with the phone company from Seattle to San Jose, California. I knew God had bigger plans for me.

In 1969, while still maintaining my job with the phone company, I joined the popular Edwin Hawkins Singers, a gospel choir based in the San Francisco Bay area. They recorded a song that quickly skyrocketed to the top of the national music charts and remained in the number one position for many weeks. This gospel song burst onto the secular world when it was so needed. It was the end of the turbulent '60's, the Vietnam war, protests, and protest songs. *Oh Happy Day* was the first gospel song to cross over and appear on secular music charts, and sold over a million copies worldwide. The Edwin Hawkins Singers toured throughout the United States and Europe, making numerous concert and television appearances.

The Gospel Music Association recently inducted eight music superstars into its Gospel Music Hall of Fame in Nashville, TN, including the Edwin Hawkins Singers. I was honored to accept the award on behalf of the group's induction.

In 1974, I performed as a soloist in a new musical called "Alleluia" and recorded my first solo album the following year, produced by Hal and Judy Spencer (Manna Music). Then one day, as I sat at my desk at the telephone company, my supervisor came and notified me that someone named Bill Gaither was on the phone. I fondly recall that was like saying the President of the United States was calling me! That call resulted in becoming one of the artists on Bill's new Paragon label and touring with the Gaither Trio.

By this time I was confident that God was leading me into full-time ministry. I took a leap of faith and left my job of more than 20 years with the phone company. I had thought my life was planned.... I would work 30 years at the telephone company, receive a full pension and enjoy life. But I am very happy that God had other plans. I hung up on Ma Bell and have been traveling the world full-time for more than 30 years as a 'Musicianary.'

It really doesn't matter if it is a small church, large church, concert hall, stadium, prison, nursing home, I promised the Lord I would go wherever the doors are opened. When I left the telephone company, God gave me this scripture in Matthew 6:26 "Look at the birds of the air; they do not sow or reap or store in barns, yet your Heavenly Father feeds them. Are you not much more valuable than they?" God has proven Himself true to His Word! He is faithful and supplies ALL my needs with no regular paycheck.

In l991, I was honored at the Na Hoku Hanohano Awards (Hawaiian version of the Grammy's) for my album, "Here's Lillie with a Victory Song." In 2000 was inducted into the Gospel Music Hall of Fame and have been a Dove Award nominee. God showed me His plan for my life which has included preaching the gospel and singing about the love of God in 57 countries. What a blessing! ("For God is not unrighteous to forget your work and labor of love, which ye have showed toward His name, in that ye have ministered to the saints, and do minister. Hebrews 6:10.)"

After eighteen plus years of ministry as a recording artist/evangelist, I have a treasury of memorable moments and unforgettable experiences. Some of my most cherished memories are of the earlier Gaither

Homecoming tapings. I will never forget the first time I walked into the room where a huge choir of gospel music heroes and legends were gathered.

There they were----Howard, Vestal, George, Rex, Naome, J.D. and so many others.

During the course of the taping, many humorous stories and touching testimonies were shared. Heavenly voices filled the room with familiar gospel classics and songs of praise. I laughed, I cried and I worshiped.

Now approaching the age of 70, I am often asked 'When are you going to retire?' My answer........NEVER! I want to work as long as I can. Each day I'm humbled to see how God uses me in so many different ways and in so many different places. I love the ministry God has called me to and will continue until He changes it.

I trust that we are all doing what He has asked us to do. The only place to be is in the perfect will of God. I know that whatever our age, if we are willing to do what God asks us to do, He will give us strength and stamina to keep going until He calls us home to receive our reward.

# MY STORY.....JACQUELYN HAVENS
# WHERE "GRACE" ABOUNDS

Growing up in a very large Christian family taught me the sovereignty of God and how He places us in the very circumstances which are best for us to be nurtured..... not by our standards but by HIS standards!! I was the 2nd oldest child of the large Grace family ......9 girls and 5 boys. Most of us grew up in the small town of Madeira, Ohio, suburb of Cincinnati. In 1946, Dad Grace bought a large rambling three-story house, part of which was built before the Civil War. We found out later from the names carved on the 3rd floor ceiling beams that this home belonged to the DeMar family, the first settlers of Madeira. The boy's Dorm was on the 3rd floor and in the winter, they'd play basketball up there and the whole house seemed to rock back and forth with the thumping of that ball.

Our brother, Daniel, age 7 or 8 spotted the large empty lot next to our old house on the hill, so he started exploring each day digging for treasure. Pretty soon, he hit something suspicious and took the artifacts home to show Mom and Dad, who promptly took them to the City Council. They were informed that the land was an ancient Indian burial ground, and to tamper with a grave site was a federal offense! (no one was arrested)

I remember one time, Dad hired a cleaning lady to help out, and after just 2 days, we found her crying... she just threw up her hands and said, "Every time I spend 4 hours cleaning this house, it gets messed up in fifteen minutes with all these kids...I just can't take it any more... She quit!

Our Dad and his four Grace brothers inherited the family business... the Willson Dairy on Reading Road in

Cincinnati, Ohio, and believe me, he needed a dairy to feed our family!! Dad told us the Willson Dairy slogan was, "You can whip our cream, but you can't beat our milk!"

Our parents were very non-materialistic and gave away much money to missions. Instead of buying nice furniture, they sent us kids to Greenwood Hills Bible Camp in Pa, or to Blue Ridge Bible Conference in North Carolina. They were also very loving to the neighbors... Like the time a widow-lady wanted to start her own business as a seamstress, our parents bought her a new electric sewing machine, even though we had an old "treadle"machine. Their motto: "It's better to give than to receive," Also, I can remember when a small, blonde neighbor girl, Billie Carter, went to my Mom and asked if she could come and live with us because her parents were splitting up. She said it was so much fun to be with the Grace family. Of course, the whole family welcomed her with open arms and she bunked in with one of our sisters for a year or two.

Dad bought a 9-passenger Chrysler from a funeral home because it had roll-out seats and we could all fit ..(almost) Many times he would surprise us and bring one of the red & white Willson Dairy trucks home with the cold metal racks in the back. All the neighbor kids would want to ride in the Dairy truck to church with us....cold seats, but a lot of fun.

We attended a Conservative Evangelical Bible Church, conducted according to a New Testament church...where the men developed their spiritual gifts by speaking at the "Breaking of the Bread" service Sunday night and Wednesday night for Bible Study. I found out later that Miss Weatherall Johnson, Founder of Bible Study Fellowship had the same church background in Plymouth, England.

One Sunday evening, a visiting preacher from Wales, named David Lawrence came to speak at our small Bible Church, when I was 7 or 8 years old. He was very short and had to stand on a wooden box to see over the podium, but He made the Gospel of Jesus Christ very clear that night. I became very worried about my eternal destiny, and while lying in bed, I asked Jesus to come into my life, and since that time I have sensed His Spirit within me. My favorite verse is, "For by grace are ye saved through faith, and that, not of yourselves, it is a gift of God; not of works lest any man should boast." Ephesians 2:8, 9.

We all enjoyed the Sunday afternoons when we entertained the visiting preachers. One afternoon we decided to take Preacher Ferguson on a special picnic. Mom made her great potato salad, and since our younger brothers had seen Mom sprinkle salt on the salad, they found the "Dutch cleanser" and sprinkled some of that in also. It was a catastrophe when we served Preacher Ferguson the salad first!

Mom and Dad Grace were Bible-believing Christians, who enjoyed their large family and took their faith very seriously and taught their children the principles of salvation through faith in Jesus Christ. Each evening we would have the Family Altar with family Bible reading and prayer, when the whole family would kneel down and pray in the living room. When my friends would be visiting, I would just hold my breath during family prayer time, but somehow they always thought this was "real cool". Dad also sent letters to all the Senators and House of Representatives, regarding abortion and pornography issues.

In 1955, my Dad and his brothers sold the Willson Dairy and Dad bought a new station wagon, filled it up, along with several other cars, the family moved to California, where he invested in a chicken ranch.

I stayed in Ohio to continue my job a G.E. and also to finalize the sale of our large home in Madeira.

While attending Wheaton College in Illinois, I heard about the S.S. North American Cruise Ship Lines that hired students from Wheaton to work on the Great Lakes all summer. When I heard that I was accepted to work, I was grateful to God that He had opened up this job to help me pay for another year of college. "His ways are past finding out." I had a fabulous time working as a waitress as we sailed from Chicago to Mackinac Island, Mich., Sioux St. Marie and Buffalo, NY, then returned to Chicago again each week. One of the college girls from St. Olaf College in Minnesota was a music major and she put together a choir and directed it for us. We also put on a Crew Show with singing and all of us dancing the Charleston. We made our own costumes!! What fun!

I attended Wheaton College and Baylor University and after working for several years, I met a wonderful man, Donald Havens, who had just returned from Army occupation of Germany in 1956. Don accepted the Lord as Savior while we were dating. He also is from a large family and we both attended small local high schools, where he was a football player and I was a cheerleader. We were married in 1957 in Ohio, and then moved to California four years later, where Don taught High School social studies for thirty-one years and I taught Work Experience in the Business Dept. for sixteen years. We have four great children and six wonderful grandchildren.

Along with the many fun and spontaneous times, there also were times of sorrow which every family seems to experience. One summer after several of the teens had joined the yearly Yosemite Bible Conference for a week of fun and fellowship, our parents received a traumatic phone call in the middle of the night, with the message

78

that three of the teens had jumped into the Merced River for a swim and two were saved by helicopters, but our younger sister, Esther was missing!! Her body had been swept down the river by an under-current due to the rains the night before. Several months later, her body was found by a fisherman. Esther was quite popular at Montclair High School and had been elected to be a Cheerleader for the coming year. At her Memorial service, many of her close friends spoke to Mom Grace of Esther's devout faith in God and asked how they, too, could have that same kind of relationship with God. We all had to experience that "My thoughts are not your thoughts, neither are your ways my ways, saith the Lord, for my ways are higher than yours." Isaiah 55:8,9 (Earth hath no sorrow that heaven cannot heal.)

His grace is sufficient to meet every need!! More than half of our large family have been fortunate enough to graduate from college with one or two degrees. Our brother, Bill, has graduated from Talbot Seminary.

The Scriptures say "You never know what a day will bring forth". In August, 2000, I had the scare of my life when a biopsy showed carcinoma and the Dr. told me I needed a hysterectomy as soon as possible. My comfort came directly from God in Psalms 91:1  "He that dwelleth in the secret place of the most high shall abide under the shadow of the Almighty." My dear children were there for me 24/7 with their prayers. Two weeks later, the lab reports showed not sign of invasion. How God does answer prayer!! Every family member was affected differently by this family crisis. One of our daughters, Shari told me that when she was talking to the Lord the other day, she said "If there is any sin in my life talk to me about it, but please don't take it out on my mother!"

We then discussed how God is so wondrously all-wise with unconditional love and that He is able to challenge every family member in a different way according to his or her need at the time...What a sovereign Heavenly Father we have!!

Adversity is God's way of training us for service. If we are not prepared to train, we cannot expect the blessings of a mature relationship with Him.

Don and I have been blessed over the years to open our home to Campus Life during the time the children went to Upland High School. More recently, we have the privilege of hosting a weekly Prayer and Bible Study in our home for couples from church. It is rewarding to share the love and joy of Christ as we serve Him.

For the past fourteen years, I have enjoyed being in leadership in Community Bible Study, in Palm Desert, CA. This wonderful in-depth Bible Study has enriched every part of my life. When I was ill six years ago, the ladies from CBS surrounded me with love, dinners, flowers and prayers for which I am eternally grateful. I praise the Lord for His sovereignty over every event in my life. With Him nothing is coincidental and He holds every breath of life and my destiny in His hands. Everything that He allows is so that He can reveal His grace, power and mercy to me and to others. I can look forward to the future, knowing that whatever lies ahead regarding me and my extended family, He will be with me through all eternity. "May God's grace be upon all who love our Lord Jesus Christ with an undying love" Ephesians 6:24

# MY STORY... YRENA M. FRIEDMAN
## Prescription for Peace

Many people ask me the spelling, pronunciation and meaning of my name, Yrena. Yrena -Y-R-E-N-A-- is pronounced with a long "E", "rain" like from heaven, and ends with an "ah"—a peaceful sound. Yrena means peace in Greek which is ironic because it's something I always wanted in my life but never had (pause) until one day when I lost nearly everything I valued in life.

My parents named me Yrena—peace—during a similar time in their lives. You see, my dad was a Holocaust survivor, half Jewish and shipped off to one of Hitler's work camps after losing nearly everything during a bombing. During this time my mom and sister were kept out of harm's way in a farmhouse owned by a lady named Yrena until my dad escaped. My mom could have been devastated but she says she never gave up hope; she always had faith that they would be reunited—and they were. So in a way, my parents found peace in the middle of the war through the safety of the farm house that Yrena had to offer—and through their faith.

They learned the hard way that peace is not the absence of war but it is recognizing something even more precious—it is knowing that all things are going to work together for the good for those who love God and who are called according to His purpose—even in the midst of the battle.

Over fifty years later, I was also faced with an extreme hardship, a battle of my own. The circumstances were totally different but like my parents, I also found peace after nearly losing it all. Let me explain this to you.

After immigrating to the United States, my parents were determined to make something of themselves. In particular, my dad was on a mission to prove Hitler wrong by showing he was a valuable human being instead of a worthless Jew as he was always told—and my dad worked very hard. My mom helped support my dad through pharmacy school and eventually they owned a pharmacy business and were very involved in the local community and professional organizations. My Dad's "prescription for peace" was not really peace at all, but "success" in the world's eyes. All this "success" came at a cost. The entire family suffered from his lifestyle choices and he died at a relatively young age after three heart attacks.

Like a good little girl, I followed my father's footsteps and was also very determined to prove myself and live a "successful" life. I admired the positions, possessions and power my dad seemed to have. My dad made a name for himself and I was proud to be associated with him. I went to college and earned a doctorate degree also in pharmacy where I met the president of the student pharmacy association and who adored me. We got married and had healthy children together. As two professionals, we had many possessions and were very busy earning and spending money. But the more I got, the more I wanted. I was never content and often felt guilty for buying things I really didn't need.

In addition to the possessions, I became obsessed with power and position. I quickly moved up the company ladder and held leadership positions at work and in professional organizations. I thrived on recognition from others. But again, the more I accomplished, the more I needed to sustain the feeling of self-worth. I worked excessive hours at the expense of my dear family. I thought about work constantly even when I was home. I became very anxious because of all the projects and deadlines. I self-medicated with alcohol, prescription medications and compulsive shopping to help me cope with life and the feelings of emptiness inside. I had cracked several teeth in my mouth from grinding my teeth at night and took ibuprofen around the clock because of the joint aches I had all due to the stress I kept inside. But things just got worse and worse. I remember feeling like life was spinning before my eyes as if I was on a top and couldn't get off. I thought I had control of my life but the truth was that my life style had control of me.

The choices I made had finally made me who I was: a lonely, controlling and bitter person. The things I valued most in life—peace and deep meaningful relationships--seemed so distant. I was full of stress that my own family didn't want to be around me because I was so defensive and critical. We were deeply in debt because of my compulsive shopping. I was so lonely that I felt like a little bird pecking at the outside window, trying to get into the happy and playful lives of my husband and children. I knew something needed to change but kept thinking "later".

We moved to Carlsbad where I thought I would finally be happy-- living at the beach instead of the desert. After nearly 20 years of hard work I thought "I have finally arrived." I finally had the home of my dreams and was published in the peer review literature but I still remembered feeling so empty inside. I thought, certainly, there must be more to life than getting married, raising children, getting lots of stuff, only to retire some day and die. I needed a "prescription for peace". I remember asking myself "*is this all there is?*"

Shortly thereafter, my life changed drastically and quickly. My beloved husband was diagnosed with terminal pancreatic cancer and was given 3-6 months to live. One top of this, we learned that his life insurance policy had lapsed which meant I was about to lose my lifestyle of luxury and would be forced to live on half the income in a home that cost four times as much as our previous home. But my worst fear was yet to come: raising two teenagers all by myself. I never liked teenagers and my husband always promised me that he would be there to help me raise them if I would just get pregnant. I was so afraid that they wouldn't love me, that they would rebel like I did as I teenager and run away. I was afraid that I couldn't care for them the way my husband did. At the same time I was angry because I knew I would have to give up my corporate dreams which was so much a part of my identify.

I resented the fact that I was going to have to sacrifice for the sake of my children for essentially the first time in my life. I was overwhelmed. My head spun and my heart felt like it was crushed. I cried hysterically and literally collapsed to the floor. I felt like a piece of tempered glass that had just been thrown on the ground, broken into tiny little pieces never to be put back together again the same.

In my hour of desperation, I received a call from one of my girlfriends who I admired. She always seemed cheerful and content even though she had little in the way of material things, education and a career. But she had the one thing I always wanted but never had so far: peace. I remember being angry at God and asked my girlfriend "why is God doing this to us?" All she could do at the time was reassure me that God had a plan and purpose for our lives but that our ways are not His ways. She encouraged me to keep seeking God and to trust in Him.

What she said began to make sense to me but for the most part I still thought I was in control and knew it all. I told myself that I could just start life over: sell the house and move into a smaller place, keep working away, get remarried and raise the kids the best I can.

A few days later I confidently told another friend, "Oh well. Rick is going to die but at least I'll see him in heaven some day". I was not prepared for what I heard next. My dear friend had the courage to tell me the truth: I was not going to heaven. I was stunned because I thought I was a good person; after all I never killed anyone.

- Over time, she told me that the Bible says God hates sin: lying—even "white" lies, telling just part of the truth or embellishing the truth. I had done a lot of this to get ahead in the world. stealing regardless of the value. dishonoring our parents. I was guilty especially as a teenager!
- Coveting—materialism and greed which was so much a part of my lifestyle—and not just the really bad sins like murder and adultery.
- She said that the Bible says God doesn't just hate the things we do, but those wrong attitudes of the heart such as being angry with someone without just cause, unforgiveness and pride. Boy, was I prideful and always thought I knew it all.

I learned that committing sin makes us a sinner – not a good person—and that sin separates us from God. I thought, "oh wow". This separation from God was the source of my lack of peace. She told me that the wages (or consequences) of sin – just one sin-- is death. All my good works didn't make up for the sin in my life. I needed to repent and believe in God. In short, if I didn't stop sinning, I can expect worse things to happen. I deserved to die because of the choices I had made. These words pieced my heart.

I asked her how she knew these things and she told me that God says so in the Bible and to read it for myself. I even argued with her, but she stood firm. I eventually asked her what I need to do to make sure I'm going to heaven.

She told me that I needed to repent—turn away--from my selfish and sinful way of living and instead, turn to Jesus and put my trust in Him. The Bible says without repentance, there is no forgiveness of sins. I learned that the Bible says that it is the blood that makes atonement (covers) for the soul. My girlfriend explained that Jesus is God and He died on the cross and shed His blood to pay the price for our sins. Jesus rose again to prove that He has the power to overcome the death of sin. She said that there is no other way; only Jesus is way, the truth and the life and no one comes to the Father except through Him. She said it was my choice: my blood or His.

I never heard this before even though I was raised in a church. I was never taught to read the Bible for myself before and didn't have much time now. I needed real answers and more evidence. So I went to another girlfriend who told me essentially the same thing. Then I went to a third friend who confirmed what the other two had already told me: I needed to admit I was a sinner and need the savior—Jesus-- or I can expect the due penalty of sin which is separation from God forever.

I was desperate to have a new life. I was willing to do whatever it took to have peace in my life and to make sure I would see my husband in heaven again someday. My head was spinning and I couldn't believe that I was wrong all these years about heaven and hell. I had so many questions.

My one girlfriend even drove out from Colorado to be with us and answer questions that I had. She left me some biblical materials and encouraged me to read them for myself. These materials explained in simple terms what all my friends had said about sin and God's plan of peace for all of our lives. It all made sense to me and I was finally ready to give up control of my life and pray to God to forgive me and help me change. I finally cried out to God, accepted His forgiveness which changed my life forever.

Now, I finally had what I always wanted in life: perfect peace. This peace is different. This is not a peace that I am going to get everything I want in life. This is a peace knowing that I have been made right with God not by my works but because of what Jesus did on the cross. And when I die, I will go to heaven.

Also, I have peace knowing that no matter what happens in life, God loves me and he has a plan and purpose for my life. This peace that I am trying to describe surpasses all human understanding and cannot be comprehended unless you have discovered it for yourself.

The next couple of months were the best time of my marriage. My husband, Rick and I began praying together openly to God as if we were talking to a friend. We started reading the Bible with the children every day. We agreed that if we say God is number one in our lives, we needed to prove it in our actions. I was fascinated by reading the Bible, developed a hunger for the Word of God, and applied what I read to make changes in my life as God revealed the need.

Instead of living to please myself, my mission became to please God by really loving and respecting my husband instead of trying to control and change him. I stopped nagging, arguing and complaining which grieves the Holy Spirit—God's work in our relationships. Because of my relationship with God and by reading the Bible, there was a transformation in my mind, a change in my attitude and outlook towards life. Instead of dwelling on the negative, I trained my mind to focus on what is good, pure and lovely in people, situations and even myself. God gave me an attitude of gratitude. Instead of focusing on what I don't have, I am thankful for what I do have in the way of my relationship with God, my family and friends. God has already given me everything I need for life by what Jesus did, my faith, food and clothing. The joy of the Lord Jesus became my strength.

Because of God's strength in me by the power of the Holy Spirit, I eventually stopped working and drinking obsessively, and taking other drugs. God helped me to stop wasting my time shopping excessively and start using my time and energy to serve my family and friends, attend church and Bible studies. I started serving in the church and less fortunate people in the world. My outlook is positive because I believe in God's word—the Bible—and all of His promises: His blessings and his curses. Judgment begins with the Church—those who profess to be followers of Jesus. I believe and have experienced first hand not only God's judgment but that all things work together for the good, for those who love God and who are called according to his purposes. God truly made me a new creation from the inside out. I still stumble at times but am quicker to confess, repent and ask God and others for help.

My old hardened heart which was full of hurt and bitterness slowly softened into a heart full of love, joy and compassion for others. In time I overcame bitterness towards others by praying for them, blessing them and doing good for them. I truly learned to love my enemies, those who had intentionally hurt me over the years.

Each day I chose each day to get better other instead of bitter by letting go of things I can't control, not getting easily offended and holding grudges. God redeemed and restored my relationship to Him and all of my loved ones over time. My husband passed away but I have a relationship with a heavenly husband who will never leave or forsake me and I have a relationship with my two children who are now 18 and 20 that is immeasurably more than I could ever dream or imagine.

I've been a pharmacist for nearly 25 years and can honestly say there is no better way than God's way. I discovered that the prescription for peace is not in pills, possessions, professions, positions, power or even people. The prescription for peace is from the Great Physician: Jesus Christ; having a personal relationship with Him, through prayer, reading the Bible and obeying what it says. It is through Jesus that we have peace that surpasses all understanding.

Are you searching for peace? Do your possessions or your profession leave you empty, always striving for more? Are you obsessed with things that drive you when needs are not met? Have you lost a loved one? Are you suffering from loneliness and heartache? Do you hear God calling you to Him right now? If you seek the peace I've spoken about, if you are ready to repent and seek God's forgiveness pray along with me in your heart.

Dear Heavenly Father,
I am so sorry for my sins. I do believe that Jesus is the Son of God and that You died on the cross to pay the penalty for my sin.

Please come into my life, forgive my sin and make me a member of Your family. I now commit to turn from going my own way. I want You to be the center of my life.

Thank you for Your gift of eternal life and for your Holy Spirit, who has now come to live in me.

I ask this in the name of Jesus. Amen.

If you just prayed this prayer with me and meant it, congratulations, you are now a child of God! Jesus, the Prince of Peace, has paid the price for your sins. May His peace be with you as you start your new journey.

# MY STORY... JUDY DE YOUNG

Never in my wildest dreams could I have imagined what God would do in my life. Growing up in Miami, Florida, the middle child of three sisters and one brother, we were a very quite family. My mother firmly believed children should be seen not heard.

Because of my Dad working nights at the Miami Herald (newspaper) my Mom was a strong influence in my life. We walked to church Sunday morning and night, and also Wednesday night. My Mother was very active in our church and encouraged us to do the same.

When I was around 10 years old, we went with my Mother to deliver some Sunday school materials to a lady in her class. While waiting in the car, we noticed two young men doing lawn work in the yard. All of a sudden, they started doing acrobatic tricks and entertaining my sisters and I. This was my introduction to my future husband, Jimmy DeYoung.

I accepted the Lord at the age of 11 and was baptized with my older sister. I remember that night not only for the spiritual exercise but also because my mother admonished me that there be no "messing " around while we were getting ready to be baptized as this was the "most important" decision in our lives, to that point in my young life.

Four years later I had my first date with Jimmy, of course, it was a church fellowship, and that night we went along with my sister and her date. This began a long relationship that has lasted over fifty years now. We dated for three years and then with Jimmy going into the Air Force and being so far away for a year, he asked my Dad if we could get married.

To our surprise my Dad said "yes". We found out later that my parents thought we would run away and get married, so better to have a nice church wedding, with a good solid beginning. We were young, I was 17 years old and Jimmy was 18. Today that seems very young but we were committed to each other, and we both had a special comment to the Lord.

From the very beginning we realized that God had a plan for our lives. Maybe we didn't do everything right but we could always go back to the Word and know that He was in control.

The first couple of years of our marriage we lived in Del Rio, Texas. This was a long way from Miami, so it wasn't so easy to get mad and run home to Mommy. We had to work things out. In our first year we had Jimmy, our oldest son, the second year we had Leslie our oldest daughter.

These were hard years financially, emotionally and learning to live together. I remember roasting some pheasants Jimmy had shot while hunting. I did not realize you were supposed to remove the pellets from the bird first. I was so proud of only spending $12.00 per week for groceries and only learning later that my Dad thought we were starving to death. It was interesting to see how he would find reasons to send us money.

Jimmy decided at the end of his four years in the Air Force, though he worked in Armed Forces Radio, a job that he really loved, to get out of the Air Force. His decision was based on the fact that a great deal of his tine was spent overseas alone. We had a two year old boy and nine month old daughter and after much prayer decided God was calling him into the ministry.

At that time in our lives we started to watch the Lord provide for our needs. It was at this time, with the help of "Uncle Sam" who would provide the funding for Jimmy's schooling that the Lord showed us He would take care of our every financial need. We moved to 'Tallahassee, Florida and Jimmy entered Florida State University. Our parents were very supportive and helped as much as they could, again a sample of God's provision for our family.

While at Florida State I worked fulltime at a bank and Jimmy worked two part-time jobs and went to school fulltime. Through working at a church in a small town in southern Georgia we realized we needed to get some Bible training, somewhere, in a Bible school. Jimmy, while holding down a fulltime job, was used by the Lord in 22 Revival meetings in that one year.

It was through one of these meetings we met Dr. Fred Brown. He had a big influence on our lives by advising us to go to Tennessee Temple University for the needed Bible training. During this period of time we had our third daughter, Jodi. It was during this time we became focused once again on what God's plan for our lives was to be. Sometimes we get too busy, self-centered, and Satan tries to change your focus but God is faithful and never leaves us even though we pull away to try to do things "on our own".

God has, through my entire life, put special women in my life. The first was my Mother, who is now with the Lord. She was always supportive, most of the time from afar as we have lived in different parts of the country and the world. Never once did I hear her complain about my being away from her. Always encouraging!

While I was working the three years in Tallahassee there was a lady, who worked with me, who was such an encourager. She truly cared for me, and our family. She taught by example. She always talked so positively about her husband and family never negative. This was a great lesson to this young wife and mother.

When we went back to school the second time at Tennessee Temple, we now had three children, and again God provided for us with a new home through the VA loan we were able to get because of Jimmy's service in the military. Jimmy had a job putting Tennessee Temple's radio station on the air and working with the young peoples group at Highland Park Baptist.

I was able to find a job the first day I applied. This allowed me to get my "PhT" while we were at Tennessee Temple, "pushing hubby through", PhT. God supplied our needs through Sunday school classes, friends who would bring groceries over and one special family who invited our family over many Sunday nights after church for waffles and creamed beef. I am sure God has a special crown for these people. I certainly learned the "gift of hospitality" from this family. We learned that it doesn't matter how much you have, or don't have, you can always share. You never know how this affects other lives.

Jimmy had a men's singing group called the Collegians that traveled and sang, gave testimonies, weight lifting exhibitions in churches and high schools when you could actually get into public high schools. We still hear of people getting saved during these meetings and giving their life to the Lord for full time service.

My part in Jimmy's ministry was to keep the home fires burning, learning that the work at home with our kids, in God's eyes, was just as important as being on the front line so to speak. I always tried to make sure my attitude and spirit was right so that I would convey to our children that I was happy in the roll God had given me. We enjoyed our time at school and made precious friends that we still keep in touch with around the world, especially our group of Collegians who, like us, now are grandparents and loving it.

While at Temple, three particular men came to speak at various times. The first was Harry Bollback, who preached at our annual Missionary Conference. I think Jimmy and I were probably the first ones down the aisle to dedicate our lives to missionary service. Our goal was to go to Brazil with Word of Life but first we had to finish school.

The second man to come along was Col. Jack McGuckin, missionary to Peru, from Word of Life. Jack was a great missionary speaker. He and his dear wife Gertrude became some of our best friends. Then came Jack Wyrtzen, Founder and Director of Word of Life who invited us to come to Word of Life for the summer. These three men had a life-long influence on my life because of their wives.

After loading up our three year old station wagon, we traveled north to Schroon Lake, New York, which was a major step of faith because I had never been farther north than Indiana. It never occurred to me not to go because it was so clear this was where the Lord was leading.

As a parent, grandparent and great grandparent now, I look back and see how hard that must have been for my parents to see me move so far away. Yet they never complained, they set a great example for me to follow.

While serving at Word of Life, three great women, had a great influence my life. They were Marge Wyrtzen, Millie Bollback and Gertrude McGuckin . Marge, Millie and Gertrude all became very close friends and all three built into my life as the Bible tells us the older women are to do.

I'll never forget how Marge was such a help to me at the time of the birth of Rick, our fourth child. The hospital where our youngest son was born was 35 miles from where we lived.  When I went down for a doctor's appointment the doctor advised me to stay in the area. I was already in labor. So I decided to go to the shopping mall and just by chance I ran into Marge.

She and Jack had a day off and were there doing some shopping. Marge insisted on taking me out to dinner (although Jack ate most of my dinner). They then delivered me to the hospital where our second son Rick was born.

We bought a house in Schroon Lake thinking this was where we were going to be for the rest of our lives. We loved being there, making many lifetime friends and sitting under the teaching of great Bible teachers. It was a wonderful place to raise our children and they have great memories of Word of Life.

However, we were not to stay at Word of Life, for God had different plans for our lives. In 1976 Jimmy ran for school board in Schroon Lake and won. At the time the Christian Freedom Foundation was trying to encourage Christians to get involved in voting, but also to run for public office. We felt led by the Lord to leave WOL and become involved in this movement.

While trying to get Christians to run for office, a group of pastors encouraged Jimmy to run for Congress. This was not a "highlight" in my life. I really didn't enjoy "politics" although I believe Christians should be very involved in the political arena. I felt then and still do that Jimmy's call to the ministry of preaching was the most important call on his life, and mine. I did follow him though in this political venture and supported his decision.

We gave it all that we had, until God clearly showed us He wanted us back in ministry. I believe God works through the wives, if we can only be submissive to His will. I have learned to be patient and wait. We went back to WOL for three more years before God moved us yet again through some events in our children's lives. I am sure God was not happy with these events and we were devastated but God had another direction for us to go.

We moved to Virginia and stayed with some dear friends while we were praying for wisdom and direction.

Through two Christian men God brought along another opportunity for ministry. Back to radio and in the Number one media capital of the world, New York City. Jimmy was made Vice President and General Manager of New York City's first fulltime Christian radio station, and I was his secretary.

Because the radio station had been previously owned by a Jewish newspaper, we were directed by the FCC to carry 6 hours a day of Jewish programming. At first we were disappointed but then we realized the real reason we were there. Once again God was changing our direction. We developed good friendships with our Jewish programmers who were mostly orthodox Jewish men and women.

Because of our work with the Jewish community, the Israeli government gave Jimmy a trip, all expenses paid, to Israel. He was so excited when he returned that he said we were moving to Israel. I did not feel peace about moving. Jimmy said we would not go unless I had complete peace that was what we were to do. I guess it was a fear of moving so far away but it took five years for me to get that peace.

We were taking a walk around our neighborhood one afternoon and I just felt a perfect peace about moving to Israel. To quote Samuel in I Samuel 15:22, "it is better to be obedient than to offer sacrifice". I do have a desire to please the Lord and I had let my fear take over my life.

When we started doing deputation to go to Israel, God worked all our problems out .One of our good friends was the past Director of the Government Press Office and was very instrumental in helping us to get press credentials. Of course we had worked with him at the radio station and he knew Jimmy was truly a journalist also. As Christians we had to have a vocation that no Israeli could do to stay in the country.

Our ultimate desire was to start a church and continue in communications. We arrived in Israel 4 days before the Gulf War in 1991. We were so excited to finally be in Israel but at the same time a little apprehensive. Jimmy had been speaking at a Bible School in Paris and we were able to get on the last plane flying into Israel before the war. No other American airlines flew into Israel until after the war. I think everyone thought we were a little crazy but we had a perfect peace about being there.

Friends met us at the airport and took us to their home in Tel Aviv for breakfast. They told us what preparations we must make in order to be ready for the possibility of war. They told us we needed a "sealed room" in our apartment, to get only food in cans and have a water supply in glass containers. In addition, we must get "gas mask" that would be issued by the Israeli government.

We finally arrived at our little apartment that we had rented sight unseen and proceeded to fix up our "sealed room" as well as making the other preparations for "Scud" attacks from Iraq. On our fourth day in Israel we were finally able to get our gas masks from the Ministry of Interior and that very night we heard the first of 39 sirens sound for incoming scuds.

We rushed to get into our sealed room where I was to get the gas mask ready as Jimmy would seal the door behind us so that no gases could reach us. While Jimmy was sealing the door he turned to see me in my gas mask and told me I looked like a "blond-headed anteater". Just as he was sealing the door the phone rang. It was a call from our daughter Jodi who was in Chattanooga. She told us she was watching CNN and that a Scud was on its way to Jerusalem. Jimmy told her he knew that and had to go right then.

We were very afraid, not knowing the language or very many people. That first attack may have lasted for only a half hour or so but we sat in our sealed room, with gas masks on, for almost five hours. The only reason we did not sit there longer was that we heard the singing of birds out side our window. We thought if birds were still alive and singing then there must not be any danger of poisonous gasses in the area that could harm us.

One time we were on a bus with about ten other Israelis and the siren went off, the bus stopped and we all just waited. Because of all these situations we pretty much bonded with our neighbors. They couldn't believe we would remain in Israel with this war going on. This allowed us the opportunity to share with these Jewish friends about the reason for us being in Israel, the story of their Messiah, our Lord and Savior, Jesus Christ.

After about two months of carrying our gas masks around and staying in our sealed room during the 39 Scud attacks on Israel, at the direction of Saddam Hussein, we were able to get on with somewhat of a normal life in our new "home land". We started making some friends and searching for a place to attend church. This led us to a small Bible study in the home of a couple who would become not only dear friends but partners in ministry as well.

To make a long story short, we were able to work with several couples in the Bible study to develop a plan for establishing a church. The lessons I had learned from those three friends at Word of Life, Marge, Millie and Gertrude, I was able to use to encourage two young ladies to help us move ahead with the beginning of a small church in Jerusalem.

We were able to help start the church with two other couples, six people, and the first church meeting we had thirteen in attendance. We thought that was great. Jimmy and two other men shared the preaching each week and I joined with the other ladies to watch the children during the services, prepare snacks for after the service each week and be a faithful member of the congregation. The church today is now running around 350.

During our second year in Israel, Mart DeHaan of Day of Discovery television came to Israel and asked Jimmy to co-teach on the program with him. The Lord had opened a whole new ministry to us, all because of obedience to Him. Many people have asked me what my part in the Day of Discovery production is and I guess I would have to say "it is to help in whatever way I can".

Usually I handle wardrobe (ironing shirts, etc.,) and watching over equipment when everyone else is occupied. I also do make-up for Jimmy. Most of the time I am the only female in the crew but it has been a wonderful experience to work with the Day of Discovery team. As we travel literally around the world we run into people that have seen the programs that Mart and Jimmy have made in not only Israel but Egypt, Jordan and Turkey.

Our ministry with Day of Discovery has taught us how to do our on video ministry as well. We now produce some of our own videos with our son Jim doing the camera work, and in fact, he is the "whole production team", which is usually a nine-man crew. Jim is even the "post production" team as well; he does all of the editing for the final product, of course under the "direction" of his Dad.

Our children are all involved in our ministry, which just keeps growing. With Jimmy and me traveling all the time we could not do our ministry without the help of our ministry team made up of all four of our children each with different responsibilities. Our oldest daughter Leslie is in charge of running the home office and fulfillment. That means she is the one that gets all of our materials out the door to our supporters.

Our youngest son Rick is the person to watch over the financial part of the ministry. He is the one that keeps me, and his Dad, from over spending and making certain that all the bills are paid. Jodi servers as her Dad's Administrative Assistant, which means she takes care of our schedule and travel arrangements, plus whatever else her Dad tells her he may need. The Lord helped us to raise four wonderful children with not only a spiritual background but a love for ministry and a great work ethic.

God has used so many Christian women in my life. I think throughout my life with its "normal" ups and downs, good times and not so good times I have always had someone (who I will call an "encourager") to help me along. I am sure they were all from the Lord. I needed that encouragement as I have a husband who has so much energy, so many ideas and a desire to conquer the world for the Lord. I thank the Lord for these women, for my husband and my family and for our ministry.

I strive to be that woman for those younger than me both married and single. I also speak to ladies at church groups and to the young women at bible schools. I share with ladies and young women my testimony and address some of the problems I see today, such as improper dress and disrespect for older people. I also help women to know how to develop a relationship with their children, grandchildren and now even great-grandchildren, of which I now have two.

God may not have "called" me to a certain ministry but He has called me to be a faithful wife and loving mother.  I have had many good examples and I praise His name for that.

Now we are in Israel about three months a year, doing tours, television and helping with the church. The rest of the year we are traveling in churches and in conference work.  We spend about six weeks every year in foreign countries.

Never in my wildest dreams could I have imagined what God would do in my life.  God has been very good to us, in giving us four wonderful children, good health and traveling mercies.  I would not want to be anywhere else but in His perfect will for my life.

# MY STORY..... RUTH KAMENA

What a surprising phone call asking for a story of God in *my* life!! As I seriously thought of it I became more conscious of what God has done in my life in spite of me. That alone puts any worth to my story. I will first tell briefly about my background, then God's influence on my life.

Before giving "my story" I will first include my very beginning -- God's plans even before I was conceived! Ps 139:14-18 "I will praise Thee for I am fearfully and wonderfully made. MARVELOUS are Thy works and that my soul knows right well. My substance was not hidden from Thee when I was made in secret and intricately wrought in the lowest part of the earth. Thine eyes did see my substance, yet being unformed and in Thy book all my members were written which in continuance were fashioned, WHEN AS YET THERE WAS NONE OF THEM." How precious also are Thy thoughts unto me, O God! How great is the sum of them! If I should count them they are more in number than the sand!"

I was born in So. Bend, Indiana in 1917, and had one brother 4 years older than I. My father's childhood was difficult. His father had died, his mother spoke only German, and teachers couldn't communicate with her. He was expelled from school in the 3rd grade because of his behavior...He worked on farms until he had enough money to travel by "freight car tourist class" and toured most of the States. Eventually he settled in South Bend, found a factory job, met and married my mother. She was 18 and he was 30. He worked hard to provide necessities for his family. There were few "extras."

God knew I was in a home with no Bible, no prayer, no thoughts of God. My mother had some background in church but was not involved again until later in her life. When I was 3 we moved to Oakland, California. God was preparing my way! He led us to a house for rent right by a Christian family with twin boys my brother's age. They soon invited him to Sunday School. The first Sunday he came home he pointed to the sky and told me, "See those clouds up there? I heard today that is where we go when we die!" I thought, "Sunday School's not for me!! No clouds in the sky for me!"

BUT GOD sent two faithful, friendly Sunday teachers to invite "this little sister" to Sunday School...From then on Sunday became a special time in my life. I missed only for sickness or unavoidable reasons. Later I realized every day with the Lord can be a special day.

The Bible was a new book to me. I eagerly learned memory verses from little verse cards given each Sunday and enjoyed lessons from the Bible. I was elated when I earned a beautiful leather-bound Bible for reciting perfectly the whole 3rd chapter of John's Gospel. It had to be word perfect, no mistakes, recited in front of the Sunday School, standing between 2 men with Bibles checking as I quoted it! I treasured that Bible for many years, both the bound book and especially its contents.

When I was 14 my Sunday School teacher invited me to hear a preacher at the chapel (my first time attending anything but Sunday School). On the way she asked if I was saved. The first time I had to answer that question. I immediately said "Yes" but then added "I think so because I remembered others saying "on such and such a date I accepted the Lord." I knew I had responded to God's love for me when Younger, but couldn't remember "a date". I solved my problem that night! I told the Lord, "If I'm not already saved I'm claiming this night as my date!" When I was 16 I was baptized and in fellowship with the Christians at Bethany Gospel Hall.

But in my early years there was also "*another influence*" in my life ---spiritism. My father's mother was a fortune-teller, using cards. People came with interpreters as she only spoke German. One day she told her own fortune, then advised her family she would be killed in a car accident, every bone in her body being broken.. Two weeks later she stepped off a curb, a truck coming around the corner ran over her and crushed her small, short body. This happened when I was 2 days old so I never saw her.

When we moved to California my parents became more involved in spiritism. From a very young age I was often taken to "mediums" meetings. Many sincerely believed they had a gift from God. Some began their meetings with a hymn and prayer. (Very different from physic things seen on T.V. these days!) They helped people with their problems, gave advice they received from the "spirit world" Most mediums were women. The usual procedure was to put a personal item in a tray as you entered the door ....a ring, a watch, keys, anything from personal contact with yourself. The tray was then put before the medium who picked up an article and started a message to the owner before asking to whom it belonged. They often gave description and name of the "spirit" being contacted...

My mother gave "readings" to friends when I was in my pre-teens. She rolled out shelf paper on the table, held a pen, and as you asked a mental or verbal question she wrote answers. I was not allowed in the room but could see through the glass door and later saw the papers ---- the writing never resembled hers.

Sunday mornings I faithfully went to Bethany Gospel Chapel for Sunday School and the "Breaking of the Bread" service. How impressed I was as godly men worshiped the Lord's death as He had said ---"Do this in remembrance of Me." Often tears ran down their cheeks as they thanked Him for suffering on the cross for their sins. I saw such strong examples of worship! But after I went home and had dinner my mother and I would go to a meeting nearby where several "mediums" met and would give readings. All this I did with a clear conscience, (not knowing what God said about such things). I was often told my mediums I was destined to be one!

Two weeks before I first dated Henry a medium told me a young man would soon ask for a date and later become my husband, described him perfectly. At the same time God was also leading me in that direction and I had been praying about Henry!! My Sunday School teacher had advised the girls in our class to start praying for our future husbands --we didn't know who they were but God knew! I was praying "for Henry or someone just as good!: (I left it open in case God had someone else in mind!!) We dated 3 years and had 67 wonderful years of marriage before the Lord took him Home.

Shortly after we started dating, God opened my eyes WIDE about "mediums". A preacher spoke about Israel in the Old Testament as they prepared to enter the Promised Land. God warned Israel about the false gods and idol worshipers in the land. Scriptures were read such as the following that opened my eyes and heart to the terrible error of spiritism.. I had been sincerely believing in it, even as a Christian, but I had never heard any teaching about it before.

Deut. 18:9-14 When you are come into the land which the Lord thy God giveth you, you SHALL NOT learn to go after the abomination of those nations. There she not be found among you anyone who makes his son or his daughter pass through the fire, or who uses divination or an observer of times or an enchanter, a witch, or a charmer or a consulter of mediums or a wizard or a necromancer, for all these things are an abomination unto the Lord and because of these abominations the Lord thy God doth drive them out from before thee.

THOU SHALT BE PERFECT WITH THE LORD THY GOD. These nations, whom thou shalt posses, hearken unto observers of times and unto diviners, **but as for thee, the Lord thy God has not permitted thee so to do.**"

Leviticus 19:31 Regard *not them that have familiar spirits; neither seek after wizards to be defiled by them.* I am the Lord your God.

Leviticus 20:27 A man or woman who has a familiar spirit, or who is a wizard, <u>shall surely be put to death</u>; they shall stone them with stones; their blood shall be upon them.

After learning of God's judgment on such things and turning from it I *thought* I was finished with witchcraft! When I was somewhere in my mid-40's I was teaching a Ladies Bible Class and something in the lesson opened up a discussion of fortune telling. One lady emphatically insisted "it's all fake, it has no power". I had never mentioned my experiences until that day........I then emphatically warned of its reality and God's warnings. I warned against Ouija boards for children (or anyone). They are sold as games but are controlled by spirits. I heard of one person asking the Ouija board who Christ Jesus was and the puck went flying against the wall. I warned the women against fortune tellers and all forms of spiritism.

I had "stepped on Satan's toes!". A week or so later Henry and I sat in our living room, the rest of the family was sleeping. I was on the couch with by back to the front window, Henry was across the room in a chair facing, reading. I could see through the dining room into the kitchen. I suddenly heard water running at the kitchen sink. Looking up I saw a woman getting a drink of water. She then walked out of my sight toward the bedrooms. I know no one was there. I knew it was a spirit! I talked to Henry to be sure I was awake, not telling him what I was experiencing. Suddenly the woman appeared again getting another drink. All at once, I *very positively thought* "That's my cousin Beatrice". How did I know that??? Not from what I *knew* . I knew I had a cousin much older than I named Beatrice. Her father was my mother's brother, a successful business man much older than my mother. That's ALL I knew about her! Being in California since I was 3, I never saw her or had any contact with her, I could not have picked her out in snapshots my mother might have had. My mother had little correspondence with her brother. She had been in close touch with her parents, her sister and family and some close friends but not her brother.

I was almost angry with God! I just taught against this-- that it is of Satan! "God where were You that You allowed Satan to enter my mind this way?" The next morning my mother phoned. She had received a phone call the night before that Beatrice had died!! I didn't tell my mother what had happened. She knew I had turned away from spiritism and might have been glad I had the experience.....

God gave me an answer! The Holy Spirit kept reminding me of I John4:4 "Greater is He that is in you than he that is in the world." I was confident God allowed this that I might experience the power Satan has to reach my mind, but also to remind me I have a Greater Power than Satan that can also speak to me--- His Holy Spirit!!! Before the Lord's crucifixion Jesus told His disciples the Holy Spirit would come. He told the disciples the Holy Spirit would speak to us through **the Word** and bring things "to our minds".

John 14:16-25 The Comforter, who is the Holy Spirit, whom the Father will send in my name, He shall <u>teach</u> <u>you</u> all things and <u>bring all</u> things to <u>your remembrance,</u> whatsoever I have said unto you.

Several years later I was, sitting opposite the back door in our mobile home reading and fell asleep.    I wakened suddenly as I heard the back door open; a tall man wearing a brilliant green jacket was leaving, closing the door behind him.  I knew no one was there but rushed to look anyway....there was no one there. Again, Satan attempting to intrude my mind. How great to know God is always with me and "greater is HE that is in you than he that is in the world".......

Satan is infiltrating minds today.    The "physic influence" is evident in television, movies, "religious" programs and literature.  God is a Spirit and we should worship Him only in spirit and in truth.  What is our guide?  When is it the Holy Spirit or when is it the spirit of Satan?  The Lord Himself taught the disciples when in the upper room before His crucifixion.  He told them of the coming and the work of the Holy Spirit. (John, Chapters 14-16)

John 14:17-17 "I will pray the Father and He will give you *another Comforter,* that He may abide with you forever, even the Spirit of Truth, whom *<u>the world cannot</u>* *<u>receive</u>* because it seeth Him not, neither knoweth Him, but ye know Him for He dwelleth *with you and shall be in you".*

John 15:26  "When the Comforter is come, whom I will send unto you from the Father, even the Spirit of truth, who proceedeth from the Father, **HE SHALL TESTIFY OF ME"**

John 16:7-11 (The threefold work of the Holy Spirit toward the world)

John 16:13  "When He, the Spirit of truth is come **HE WILL GUIDE YOU INTO ALL TRUTH, FOR HE**

**SHALL NOT SPEAK OF HIMSELF,** but whatever He shall hear that shall he speak and He will show you things to come. **HE SHALL GLORIFY ME** for he shall receive of mine and shall show it to you.

The test? Is the Lord Jesus getting the glory and preeminence? The Spirit is often emphasized today and given the preeminence. Little or nothing is said about the Lord Jesus Christ, except to close a prayer with 'in Jesus name' (not Lord Jesus, or Jesus Christ, *only* His earthly name - Jesus).

A second scripture that guided much of my life was the advice given by the Lord's mother, Mary, recorded in John 2:5 I was impressed in Sunday School with the miracle at the wedding at Cana of Galilee when they ran out of wine. Mary, Jesus' mother, told the servants, *"Whatever He says to you---DO IT!"* When the Lord told the servants to fill six big water pots with water (about 25 gallons each!) they DID IT ---no questions. Wine was needed, not water, but the water changed to wine. The ruler of the feast questioned why the bridegroom saved the "best wine" to the last, it was always served first........

"WHATEVER HE SAYS - DO IT" became a "way of life" to me. So often I did what I was asked to do, feeling incapable, unqualified, insecure, but God always guided and I learned to do by 'doing'.

I was 17 when a new work started in West Oakland (Market Street Gospel Hall) I was asked to teach the youngest class and play the piano for Sunday School and the other meetings! "Teach" and "play" Two things I had never done before BUT God had been preparing me. When I was about 7 my mother bought "Theodore Presser's Beginners Piano Book" for me. She knew enough to help me through the first few lessons and then I was on my own. The piano was soon my favorite "toy". I played "games" on it! My favorite game was to be 'a blind, concert pianist, playing for a large audience'. I'd close my eyes, make up music as I played from one end of the piano to the other, trusting my ears to make it sound reasonably (?) good! It taught me to play any hymn that came to mind with or without music. From this start at Market Street and later in other assemblies I have played for Sunday School and other meetings.......'Whatever He says, DO IT"

John 2:5

The other request was to **teach Sunday School**. My high school ambition was "to teach"--High School math (Algebra, Geometry, Trigonometry, Calculus) that never happened, there was "no money for college". But God had already started a "Teachers Training Course". The teenage girls in Sunday School had a wonderful godly teacher ---Hannah Anderson. Besides teaching us she also started teaching us "to teach". Each month one girl would sit in on a Sunday School class of young children, observing how it was taught.......The next Sunday she taught our class as if we were the "little kids" and presented a lesson accordingly. Good practice!! Then I started teaching those "little ones" at Market Street. A few years later I was teaching teenage classes ---because "there was no one else" for them.

Hannah Anderson then came to help at Market Street Gospel Hall and started a ladies weekly Bible Class which I attended. When the war started she went back to work, first informing me I would have to teach the ladies Bible class she had started!! I was about 22 at the time. Did I ever start "digging deep" into the Word then! I remembered not only John 2:5 "Whatever He says to you, do it!" but also experienced John 14:26 "The Holy Spirit will teach you and bring all things to your remembrance".

God's plans for me at Market Street also included Henry, my future husband.  (A terrific plan!)  He was also willing to leave our larger home assembly and work in West Oakland.  He became the song leader, taught Sunday School, preached, etc...We worked together for the Lord from then on.

On one occasion after I was married I attended a Sunday afternoon Ladies Missionary Meeting at Fairhaven Bible Chapel in San Leandro.  The meeting started on time but the speaker hadn't arrived!  She was expected soon, coming from San Francisco.  One song after another was sung as we waited.  The women in charge finally decided something had to be done besides "another song".  To my dismay one of them left the platform, came to me and asked me to "fill in with something 'till the speaker arrived!!!"  (There it was again, "What He says unto you ---DO IT!)  I responded with "sing one more verse as I collect some thoughts!!" I don't remember the exact verses the Holy Spirit laid on my mind, it was in Philippians or Colossians, you can always talk a lot about verses there!!  I began---went on ----and on---still no speaker and finally asked "Shall I keep going on ??"  They then decided to close the meeting.  As refreshments were served the speaker arrived!  She had looked for the MacAuthur Blvd. address in Oakland instead of San Leandro - did a lot of extra driving and inquiring!  Why did God allow it to happen? I don't know.  I do know I learned again that 'Whatever He says-DO IT!  He will give the needed help.

What if it seems **impossible?**  In 1955 friends came from Los Angeles to Oakland for a November conference. During their stay they mentioned plans they were making for Vacation Bible School the next summer in So. Calif.  We, in turn talked about our weekly "craft night" etc.  They made a casual statement--- "We could use you at Bible School!"  The next day they gave a firm invitation......would we come? Henry to do the speaking and I would do the crafts. We agreed. "Whatever He says, Do it!"

Before we left for Bible School Henry had a fall, broke his heel. He was released from the hospital, with crutches, the day we were to leave. We packed the car, clothes, craft supplies, 3 children (15, 12 and 7), crutches ourselves and took off. At Tracy, A short ways out of Oakland, the car began to steam. When we stopped and put water in the radiator the station attendant asked how far we were going. When we said "Los Angeles" he said "You'll never make it!" We *repeatedly* stopped all the way to L.A. for Ted (our oldest) to fill the radiator and we made it! In L.A. a friend adjusted something on the motor and we had no more trouble all the two weeks. After Bible School we started back over the Grapevine and the motor again began to steam. Ted again put water in the radiator from service station to station. We made it home! The next day the garage man said "It's impossible you made a round trip to L.A. There's 2 cracks in that block" BUT GOD knew it was too late to make other plans for Vacation Bible School --only 2 days and so much depended on our being there! Scripture again was proved -- GOD CAN do the impossible!

All through High School MY plans were not God's plans! Math was my favorite subject. MY plan was to teach High school math-----God closed that door---there was no money for college! And I was only 16 when I graduated (15 when I entered my senior year). The Oakland public school system had Merritt Business College available with a complete choice of business subjects. (THAT WAS GOD'S PLAN!) I attended there all day, every day, for 2 years, preparing for any type of office work. GOD'S PLAN was to use that office training all the rest of my life for Him (as well as the early "teaching" experience, and my "amateur" music ability)........all in serving Him. As soon as I turned 18 the school sent me on an interview and I had a bookkeeping job in a Custom Brokers office in San Francisco.

(My job in San Francisco had an added enjoyment ---the Oakland/S.F.bay Bridge was being constructed as I commuted for 2 years on the ferries. I watched them string all those high cables that hold the bridge up!)

I worked 13 years in the office of the Home of Peace of Oakland, a 3 story Missionary Service built around 1892, originally to care for retired missionaries. Around 1942 it became a service to missionaries coming and going from their mission fields. Missionaries from many fundamental denominations stayed there at minimal cost. The 2nd and 3rd floors were rooms and baths. The main floor had large living rooms, dining room, kitchen, etc. A warehouse provided packing, crating, etc. I did the bookkeeping, billing, booked passage for missionaries, etc. A wonderful opportunity to serve the Lord's servants on the mission fields. What wonderful fellowship as we served God's servants.

In 1969 I left the work at the Home of Peace and went to Western Assemblies Home in Claremont, Ca, (a home for elderly Christians)Three board members living in the Bay Area were praying about the need for a maintenance man and the Lord kept putting Henry in each of their minds. When they conferred with one another and realized all 3 had the same leading from the Lord, Henry was contacted. There it was again ---John 2:5 "Whatever He says to you, do it"---we moved to Claremont. While Henry did the maintenance, I took on the kitchen afternoon shift and prepared the evening meal for the residents. (The first supper I prepared by myself included "Cheese soufflé's" for each table!!) After 2 years the Lord led me to a job at Sunkist Growers in Ontario, CA.

I used my "office training" for 13 years at Sunkist Growers, working in exports. I already had experience with steamship companies from time at the Home of Peace. In 1982 I retired from Sunkist as manager of the export department, and again enjoyed spending more time in activities at church, the ladies Bible class, etc. until 1987.

In 1987 a new Administrator began working at Western Assemblies Home who had no bookkeeping experience. I offered to help if ever she needed it with the books. Instead I was hired to work in the office, and also do the bookkeeping. Several years later I quit working in the office but I still continue doing the bookkeeping in my own home, on my own time schedule.

A month before our 67th anniversary God took Henry to be with Himself. He was in the hospital three days, had a pacemaker put in and was to go home the next morning. Early that morning the hospital called for me to come quickly. As I entered his room he peacefully said "I'm going home! I love you!" Within an hour he was with the Lord. Before dying he peacefully informed me who should take his funeral.

God planned our last few years so well. He had individually turned our thought to moving to Western Assemblies Home. We sold our mobile home, made future funeral arrangements, and moved in, ready to face the "rest of our lives"!. Our family was favorable to our decision. After three years the Lord took Henry to be with Himself. As long as God continues to give me a good measure of health I am prepared to continue as before ---"Whatever He says, Do it!" Besides still doing the bookkeeping, I am involved in a Ladies Bible Study, playing the organ 3 evenings each week for a "sing" (the Home's "Make a Joyful Noise" group), playing the Organ at church etc. etc. God's plans for Henry's life were completed. Now the peace of God that passes all understanding keeps my heart and mind through Christ Jesus. (Phil 4:7) as I continue on until His plans for my life are also completed or until that promised "meeting in the air" for all His church.

# MY STORY..... BONNIE CARLTON

Even though my life is not 'extraordinary', I can still see that God has had His hand on it. I was born into a Christian home (albeit a rather chaotic one) in a small country town in western New York. My mother had been married before and had five children before her husband died; my father had been married before and had two children before his wife left him and their children. So, when my parents met and married they brought seven children to the marriage and proceeded to add two more, my brother and me. Our house included "mine, yours, and ours" with lots always going on!

I accepted the Lord as my Savior when I was seven years old but it wasn't until I was fifteen that I really understood what having a personal relationship with Him could mean in my life.

After graduating from high school I attended Buffalo Bible Institute in Buffalo, NY, and this is where I met my husband. We were married in 1959. Over the years God has led us to minister in many ways in the churches we've attended and my husband and I have been involved with taking trips to Haiti to help build churches and schools with Grace Mission, Haiti. What a blessing it has been to see God expand the work there and to be a part of what God is doing.

As I think back about my experiences in Haiti I am always amazed at God's goodness. Haiti is a country with so many needs – materially as well as spiritually. And yet the people I met never complained about their lack of material needs; needs I think are essential such as electricity, clean water, good roads – things we take for granted in America! The small church in Carrfour (a suburb of Port au Prince), which was the first church Grace Mission to Haiti helped to establish and build, has now grown to over 1,000 members. The pastor, Beril Louis, is also the Haitian Director of Grace Mission to Haiti and he oversees the other 28 churches affiliated with Grace Mission. God has blessed Pastor Beril with wisdom and intellect and he is committed to reaching his country with the gospel.

Every year, in September, Pastor Beril invites the Haitian pastors, deacons, Sunday School teachers and their spouses, who are associated with Grace Mission to Haiti to attend a conference at the Carrfour Church. The first conferences were held in a small compound where the Haitians all stayed together, sleeping on mats and cooking their meals over an open fire. The men had their meetings separate from the women with the women from the States teaching the Haitian women whatever the Lord had put on our hearts. It was always interesting to see how He had coordinated our thoughts as the lessons taught seemed to be a blessing and what needed to be heard.

My contribution to the teaching was to use material put out by the Bible Club Movement (which later either became Child Evangelism or became a part of that organization). They put out many children's stories that could be used like flash cards. Some of them were "The Little Boat Twice Owned", "Frannie's Nest", and "Barney's Barrel". The Haitian women loved the stories which I left there for them to use in their Sunday Schools. I later found out they passed them from one church to the other through the year. Because we had to use a translator it was interesting to see the reaction the stories got – Laughter, tears, clapping, etc. as the stories would unfold. It could be the translator was embellishing the whole thing but the ladies sure seemed to enjoy the telling. We'll never know how the stories ended up being told, but hopefully the gospel message got through.

In later years, as the mission grew in number, the ladies group was discontinued as there was not room to separate the men and women. The trips to Haiti have been such a blessing to me, just seeing how God is working in His world. His message is to all people, in all places, for all time.

Back home in Maryland where I live with my husband John, I work as a church secretary at the church where we worship. Music has always been another important part of my life, and singing along with my husband (who has a wonderful voice) has been such a blessing over the years. I also play the piano for our congregational singing as well as playing for the choir when I was in Bible School. We also have 3 children and 8 grandchildren that live close by and with all of this going on we are kept pretty busy.

Has everything always gone along with no problems? Of course not, but God has always been there and His grace is always sufficient. I guess being an optimist I've tried to think positive so even in looking back over my life I try not to dwell on those times when things weren't so good. God has been faithful and He is good and He is good all the time!

# MY STORY.....WANDA LEWARK
# GOD'S FAITHFULNESS IN MY LIFE

As I look back over the years of my life I can see, clearly, God's gentle mercies day by day. From the faithful neighbors that would take me to church as a child to the ever present Spirit of God that sustains me day by day.

I never doubted the existence of God – nor that He sent His Son to die for the sins of mankind. My doubt was that He could find anything in me that was worth saving. So even though I prayed to receive Christ as my Savior, early in my life, I wasn't able to appropriate His love and plan for me. Because of things that happened to me in my childhood I thought myself unlovable on any level.

In the early 1970s my husband and I attended the **Basic Youth Seminar.** During this week of Biblical teaching I began to understand more clearly that God had a plan for me and further that the events of my life, difficult as many were, actually molded me into the person that I needed to be. I began to see that it was the enemy of our faith that had been convincing me that God couldn't love me. I experienced tremendous freedom as a result of this teaching and returned annually for many years. I see this as the time of greatest spiritual growth in my journey with Christ.

During the mid 1970s we were forced to leave our comfortable home church. This experience caused us to seek and find God in a deeper way than we had to that point. We became dependent on Him for moment by moment leadership and provision. What an exciting time. We bonded with two other families in this endeavor and God poured out His love and grace on each of us.

120

This continued for a couple of years and then both of these families moved out of the area. What a faithful loving Father that knew our desperate need of loving friends with the same agenda – an all consuming desire to know God.

From here God took us to what we called a Word church. We were there for five years and it was as though we had gone to college to study the Bible. It was definitely a crammed course and we ate it up. We also learned about the sacrifice of praise and worship while we were there. These were wonderful days in our journey.

To fill the need for a more rounded church in our daughter's life we moved to a different church. Let me stop here to tell you, **very clearly,** God lead us in each of these moves as surely as He lead the children in the desert with a cloud and fire. This was a wonderful church and continues to be our church to this day.

In 1994 I became involved in our trade association, the Virginia Independent Automobile Dealers Association on a local level. This association monitors legislative issues, handles education/training, monitoring of business practices, legal issues and provides the forms that are necessary to operate an independent automobile dealership. I served for two years as District President. I was so glad for the opportunity to help build the image of our industry.

In 1996- I was asked to serve as a state Vice President. In 1999 I as elected as State President of this association.

While I had spent my life trying to build my husband's business and ministry, I had never anticipated being sought to fill these type positions in a predominately male industry. So I found myself surprised and fearful. I was continuously finding myself in situations and circumstances that I thought to be beyond my abilities and having to call on God to show me how and what to do.

These were exciting days! To my great surprise God had opened a mission field for me. As I went about my business, working to improve the image of our industry, people were observing my Christian walk. At each Board Meeting I was asked to pray before meetings and meals.

God was drawing them to Himself and using my testimony/lifestyle to reveal His Word. Hallelujah! What a privilege and yet frightening responsibility.

While it would take too much space to tell of all the opportunities we have had in this mission field, I would like to tell you about three men that God touched in a mighty way.

The first one was angry that a women would be even considered as president and did all he could to keep me from being elected. I never treated him differently because of that and shortly after he was diagnosed with cancer. We prayed with him and for him and just poured out the love of God for him each time we saw him. Shortly before his death we visited his home church, in a city about 200 miles away. With hugs and tears he took us to the altar where he had given his life back to Jesus. Not since he was a child had he served Christ.

The second man approached me during a meeting and literally cried out 'I can't do it'. When I asked him what he couldn't do – he said 'live the Christian life'. We spoke briefly at that time. Later at a meeting where I was not present he asked if someone would pray – saying 'all this praying really is good'. Shortly after that he also was diagnosed with cancer. During those difficult months we stayed in touch and prayed for him. Five weeks before he died he prayed to receive Christ and was gloriously saved.

Each year we hold a TIME OF SHARING on Sunday morning after our State Convention. The third man along with his wife stayed after one of these meetings and asked how they could be born again.

In part, this is especially exciting to me because each of these men were in their latter years and had lived lives centered around their own plans and yet God in His long suffering love called them unto Himself. Just to play a tiny part in that process is overwhelming to me.

After I had served as State President a door opened for a position as an officer on the National Association Board, headquartered in Texas. I served on this Board for four years moving from Secretary/Treasurer to Chairperson of the Board. Just to be clear I never sought any of these positions. God opened doors and people asked and/or elected me to serve.

The greatest honor was in 2003 when I was named as the first woman NATIONAL QUALITY DEALER. Talk about God opening doors. This is the highest honor our industry gives.

In 2005 I was appointed by the Virginia Governor to a position on the Motor Vehicle Dealer Board. This Board oversees the Motor Vehicle Dealers in the state of Virginia.

While all of these positions have been a tremendous honor it was all about Jesus. In a place where people least expected to hear the Gospel or see the love of God lived out – He called me to minister.

In 2005 my husband felt God would have him develop a devotional book based on The Prayer of Victory. He had written this prayer, based on daily praying God's Word, many years ago. So he began to refine it and to write about the value and benefit of daily devotions in the life of every believer.

Just a few months into this project my husband was diagnosed with cancer. The chemo and radiation are behind us and he is cancer free. He is currently rebuilding his strength and looking forward to getting back to writing. We were vividly reminded that each day is a blessing from God and an opportunity to serve Him. While I don't claim to understand all the reasons why things happen, I can tell you with absolute authority God is trustworthy.

We have ministered through our church, through our business, through our industry associations and also through many ministries over the years all because of God's faithfulness to us. Actually we have learned from some of God's most faithful servants how to be instant in season and out of season. We have been humbled by the privilege of calling as friends – several of God's gentle giants in the faith. Our lives are so different because of their presence, love and prayers for us. Praise be to our trustworthy Father.

God has walked with us, these many years, as we have run from Him as well as when we have run to Him, as we have stumbled and fallen, as we have complained, as we have gone through sickness and in health, as we have experienced the death of a vision, as we have moved out on what we thought to be right only to find it wasn't, and on and on. He is our faithful friend and merciful father. May our hearts burst with gratitude for all we have in Him.

# MY STORY..... JULIA FRIES

I am just overwhelmed that God has given me the opportunity to share His faithfulness to me through these many years. When Sharon asked me to do this many months ago, I was like 'there is no way' I don't do anything like this, and then as I have been praying about it, I have felt that, not in any way it would bring glory to myself or because you know me, but for you to realize the faithfulness of God to a young woman that came to know the Lord at a very young age. As I reflect back on these years I'm just going to share some of those things with you and trust that they will be used to realize just how faithful God can be when a person has yielded themselves to Him.

One of the advantages of getting older is the ability to look back at how faithful He has been over my entire life. What an incredible journey I've had with Him. I've been married to the same man for fifty-eight years, one who really loves the Lord Jesus, and because of his love for the Lord he loves me, he loves the word of God, and is a student of the word of God.

We've been so blessed to have a loving family. Our daughter is Deborah and she is married to a gentleman who's name is John. They have been so supportive of us through the years. They have three children. Julie who is in law school and lives close by us and we have the joy of having her with us on study weekends which is wonderful, and Jessie who just moved to Portland and is starting a new job. We just love Jessie to pieces, he is so kind and giving and just a wonderful young man. And Jane who just graduated from the University of Oregon and is now in counseling and loves the Lord too. We've made many plane trips over the years to stay connected and feel so blessed to have them in our lives. Then our son Daniel lives close by with his wife Linda. They have two children, Allison who is 19, and Michael who is 16 and still in high school. Since we've been retired and they are close by we have a delightful relationship with them, and have been able to share many experiences with them. So we have been blessed with the family that God has given us, and as He would want us to do we have loved, treasured and cared for them and they have been a source of joy.

My life verse has been Philippians 4:11-14. "I have learned (and am learning) to be content whatever the circumstances. I know what it is to have plenty; I've learned the secret of being content in any and every situation, whether well fed or hungry, whether living in plenty or want. I can do everything through Him who gives me strength." I can't tell you just how wonderful that verse has been as I've had to make many moves, and it's not always easy making moves but God had really wanted me to be content wherever I am, so that has been a life verse for me since we have moved so many places, but I don't want to get ahead of the story either so I'd like to share with you my thinking and have divided my story up into four seasons.

I used to do color analysis, which was a very popular thing to do back in the 70's & 80's, and how fun it was for me. I read a book about the idea that maybe some colors would look better on me than some of the other colors I had been wearing, and found out that was really true. As I shared this with some of my friends and they changed, I then had the opportunity to go beyond my knowledge and background in this and was given the opportunity to speak on this subject at many conferences, and by the time I was finished with that phase had encouraged over five hundred people to get involved in this. It was really a fun thing to do. Some of the people would come to my home and we had great times sharing in this project, dividing the colors into Spring, Summer, Fall and Winter.

As I look back over my life I look at Spring as being the very beginning as my time as a child and in the home and how the joys and heartbreaks of being in a family impacted my life. Then there is summer that is filled with tons of activity. Going off to college, perhaps getting a career, getting married and having children. A very busy time but seems like such a short time. Then came the fall in which you have a lot of changes. You see that in nature as the trees turn with beautiful, spectacular colors, then all of a sudden the leaves are gone and there are new beginnings coming, but you're not going to experience that again until Spring. Then comes the Winter, and that is the time I am in right now. Lots of changes in each season, there is beauty in every season and really there are tough times in each season. They are different for each season of life that we are in.

*Spring, Season # 1* In my spring season I was born in a small town in Pennsylvania. I was one of three children. I had two older brothers, Sidney and Jack, and my mother and father had all of their siblings in that town also. My father came from a very large family of fourteen. My mother came from a family of three sister and one brother and all of these relatives (I have ton's of relatives) would get together for family picnics and happy times in many ways.

It was during this time that my mother and father got into their own business after the war. They owned a bowling alley with pool tables and traveled with a pretty fast group, who were business owners that were friends of theirs from that town. They began partying pretty hard (as we would call it). My mother was one of the first women smokers around and that is when women did not smoke outside of the house. She smoked in the bathroom. Life really changed for us at that point. A lot of parties and for me as a child, a lot of scary times being in a house that often had people who were drinking and getting drunk.

I do remember one Christmas during this time, Christmas was always an important part for us as children, it seemed magical. I had asked for some roller skates and my brother had asked for a bicycle, well because my parents got a little confused with the drinking they got things a little mixed up and I got the bicycle and my brother got the skates. Well, I came out and got on the bicycle (it was a girls bicycle) and my brother looked so disappointed so that was not a really happy time. But we did have many happy times before my parents got into drinking and partying and before we lost everything. We had to move and they had to go to work. That was a very devastating time for my mother and father.

My mother wasn't very healthy at that point in her life. She had to work long hours in a bakery standing on her feet all day which was very difficult for her. She quit this job and went to work in a paper mill and my father went to work for a lumber company that made furniture. We had to move to a house on the other end of town, to a little house that had formerly been a one room schoolhouse.

During the time my mother was working at the paper mill, a friend of hers invited her to a Bible study and it was at this study that my mother really saw her need for a Savior and she asked Jesus Christ to be the Lord of her life. My mother radically, radically changed and my father saw the change in her and thought he should go out to the Bible study and see what all of this was about. He gave his life to the Lord at the very first meeting he attended. They started talking a lot about how the Lord was coming back and I was the only member of the family, {my brothers had made confessions of salvation at this point}, that had not and was afraid I was going to be left behind so I asked Jesus to come into my life and that was the beginning of my journey of getting to know who I had made a commitment to. The years in Pennsylvania were very interesting, life changing and really made an impact on my life that has been growing ever since as I came to know the Lord. It also changed my parents who became very loving, caring parents.

I had many school changes during these years, but the biggest change came in my junior year of high school. My parents heard about an opportunity to be involved in Christian ministries and decided that they would take that opportunity. They were invited to come to southern California and be the managers of a retirement home. It was a radical change for all of us. For me it meant going to a high school in Southern California which was very different than the schools on the east coast. The kids dressed different, they acted different. Finding friends was really hard, plus the fact that we didn't have our own home, we lived in the third part of the retirement home. All of our meals were with the people in the retirement home. They were delightful people but no young people around obviously. My mother was handling a very heavy load, managing the home plus doing all of the cooking, laundry, plus many other chores, while my father took care of the grounds and did the chauffeuring, grocery runs and so forth. My dad would also take me and some new friends that I had found to the shopping area at the mall once in a while and would patiently wait for us to finish shopping while he would have a cup of coffee or do some other things that needed to be done.

In my junior year of high school I was able to meet some friends that were very kind. A group of girls invited me to have lunch with them and they became my high school friends, the ones that I went to ball games with along with other school activities. At church there were gals that I became friends with also and was able to go with them to Christian camps in the So. California area and it was a good time to just be away from home for a little bit.

After high school I wanted to go to college but my folks really wanted me to go to Bible school for a year and then go on to college. I didn't rebel against that because there was a Bible school starting in Chicago at that time called Emmaus Bible School and after being accepted there that's where I was for the next year. During this time my mother's health was declining and the doctor recommended that they make a change so she wouldn't be doing so much work.

They got a letter from my mother's cousin, who owned a Christian printing press along with a book store. They asked my parents to work for them, so we moved back to Fort Dodge, Iowa during the summer and then in the fall I went off to Bible school. It was hard for my parents as I was the last child to leave home, and it was hard for me to be on my own as I had very low self esteem. I remember when I was growing up; having an aunt named Aunt Emoline that was very heavy and would have trouble fitting into chairs and my family would tease me that I would probably be like her. That sent me a message of determination that I would never be as big as Aunt Emoline. I just wanted to add that into my story because it is important to know that some things like that can really affect you during your life. Things like being told you are stupid or just never given the encouragement to succeed gave me mental pictures of what I would be like until God really showed me differently about my life.

*Summer, Season # 2* I am by this time off to Emmaus, and it was during this time that I really got serious about my relationship with the Lord Jesus. As I got to study and really get into the Word of God, I came to realize how much Christ had really paid the price for my redemption and He wanted me to walk with Him in obedience and not be a nominal Christian but really get to know Him. That was a real turn around in my life and as I look back, and I thank my parents for making that decision for me and enabling me to go to Emmaus.

When I went to Emmaus, they didn't have dorms and we had to rent rooms from people that had rooms available. You have to remember that time was right after World War II, and there were no apartments and that kind of thing available, so I ended up living with ten other girls and we called it Angels Flight. That was a very interesting 'growing up' time for me.

After I was there for about two weeks, there was a young man that really took an interest in me and he ended up later becoming my husband. Earl was five years older than I was, so he was pretty serious about developing that relationship and I was just out of high school and I hadn't even thought of having a growing relationship with a young man. I dated quite a bit in high school but had never told anybody that I really loved them. It was a real process for me to determine that this was the way I wanted to go. At that point it was taught to us that there was one person for you to share your life with and only one. Today I've had many opportunities to talk with young gals that really want a Godly young man to share their lives with, but that doesn't necessarily mean there is only one Godly young man, but for us at that time you can imagine the pressure to make sure you found 'the right one'. Earl and I went together for the first year and then Earl proposed to me in December. I told him I would have to think about it and asked him 'how did you know you really love me?'

I was so immature and at that time felt like putting a fleece out for God to answer was the way to find out for sure if I should marry Earl. I decided to go shopping in Chicago for a wedding dress on a particular day and told God if I found one that I liked that day then I would know that Earl was the one I should marry. Well we went to several stores and didn't find anything I liked, but then went to another store and found just the right dress. Well now I knew that Earl was the man God had for me to marry. Now that probably sounds really strange to you but it has proven to be, for us the beginning of a growing commitment to love one another for the rest of our lives and we are still in the process.

We were married in the summer of 1948, back in the town where I grew up because all of our relatives were still there. That began the journey of our lives together. We finished our time at Emmaus, and then went on to Texas where Earl got his bachelor's degree, plus his Masters, and I worked at the college during this time. We were also involved with our church during this time. Then I got pregnant with Debbie and had the joy of having this beautiful little girl that God gave us. Two years later we had a little boy that God brought into our lives; our son's name was Daniel. How I loved those years! "We lived in Texas where Earl started teaching school and he taught there for five years.

We decided during this time that it was time to make a move. We had terrible allergies and so did our children. My brother lived in California and was also a teacher. He said he would set up appointments to interview for jobs for us so that is exactly what happened. We prayed for God's direction and He provided a job for us and a place to live. At that same time my parents also moved to California and we lived by them for quite a few years.

Earl taught school in Pomona for ten years. We had fellowship with a group of Christians in Claremont and we were also involved teaching Bible studies to high school kids. I was involved with youth work and ministries with our church. It was during this time that the Lord was instilling the thought to both my husband and a man named Gary Thompson that evangelism was something that needed to be taught to our young people.

They learned of sharing their faith by using the four spiritual laws that Campus Crusade for Christ had put out and had a burden for exposing our young people to the opportunities for missions. God opened a way for this to happen by giving them a place in Mexico for training. We were able to rent a house with a million dollar view but no running water and no indoor plumbing, only out-houses. It was there that we started training young people, along with some Spanish speaking young people who also became interpreters. Gary's wife Kay and I were the cooks and these were tremendous growing days for all of us. It was during this time that we got a letter from Emmaus Bible College asking Earl if he would pray about coming back there to teach. We decided that maybe in the future that might be something that God would have us do but not at this particular time.

About six months later, Earl was the chairman of a children's home called Adelaide Home for Children. He learned from the women that had donated the money for this home that it was going to be closed down. The government was insisting that they take in emotionally disturbed kids, and this was not the reason for the home in the first place; it was intended to give homes to kids that had no home of their own and be able to teach them about the Bible. They just decided to close the home down because it wasn't meeting the needs of her goals for it. After a meeting one particular evening, Earl came home telling me that they had decided that instead of closing the home, they would like to change it into a one year school for teaching the Bible.

The board told Earl that the only way they would go ahead with this plan was if he would be a part of it. Well, my first thought was 'no way!' It meant that we would have to leave everything that was familiar and all the friends we had made over the last ten years, plus we had a very fulfilling ministry where we were. This also meant that we would have to trust the Lord for all of our financial needs, and this was just unbelievable to me, that's just not where I was at! It was a very difficult time for me and I made it a difficult time for Earl as well.

I did not want to be one of those "full time workers" that everyone would judging everything you did and every penny that was spent and I wasn't willing to do that, but as I had time to think about that, it wasn't even those things that was the big issue, it was more where I was in my walk with the Lord. It was during this time that the Lord was showing special verses and insight to Earl. He would come home saying things like "look what the Lord has shown me now!" to which my response would be "so?" Many times the four of us, Kay, Gary, Earl and I, would get together in the evening to pray about the Lord's guidance but my heart was so hard, I couldn't even really pray and talk to the Lord about it. You can imagine that it wasn't really a happy time.

One night Earl said something to me that really broke me. He said "I feel so strongly that this is what God would have us to do, that I just can't imagine what it would be like to be disobedient to Him" This was all through many tears that the Lord hit me with His thoughts that He was giving me this opportunity and if I was unwilling to do it that someone else will have that opportunity and you will miss out on the blessing. I was really fearful of not being obedient because it was so strong. That night I bowed down before the Lord in brokenness and told the Lord that I was willing to do whatever He asks us to do or go wherever He wants us to go and that I would trust Him. I can say today that I never had any doubts once that decision was made. I knew He would provide for us and that I didn't have to answer to everybody, but I knew that God would not only meet our needs but He also answered many of our wants. Anyhow, with that life really changed for us and I just wanted to share with you the faithfulness of the Lord, and that you can rely on Him for the guidance.

From this point we were able to sell our home, and as we went into look for property in the area we would be living, it was too expensive for us. We decided that we would probably have to live in an apartment. In the meantime the board had another meeting and told Earl that they were going to give each of the faculty one of the homes that was also on this property by the new school. Not only did they provide a home but all the utilities were paid for and we were abundantly provided for. On top of that, there was a doctor that had been taking care of the needs of the children in the home and he said he would like to take care of the faculty members, plus a dentist that wanted to take care of all dental needs, plus, our church gave us $50.00 a month. We were on our way...........to Culver City Bible School, one year for life! Those were ten incredible years! I grew in my walk with the Lord. I signed up for Bible Study Fellowship and that was a time for real spiritual development. We were also involved with setting up a new church in the area and those years were real growing years for me.

During the years that we were with Culver, our children Debbie and Dan finished high school, and Debbie went to junior college for a year after a year at Bible school but soon decided that was not what she wanted to do. Instead she felt the Lord calling her to work on a mission team that would be going overseas to Germany. She left us and joined International Teams. My part of that I wanted to share with you is that through the years I had really encouraged a lot of mothers to allow their kids to go on missions to serve the Lord or go to Bible school or whatever they felt the Lord was leading them into. Then it came time for our daughter to go and she was telling us that she really felt the Lord leading her to do this. When she told me this, I just sat down and started to cry. She asked me what was wrong. I said 'that means you will be gone, we may never be able to share our life together.' She said 'Mother, isn't that what you brought us up to do and said you would desire nothing more than have us serve the Lord?" I wanted to share that experience with you because sometimes it's easy for us to encourage others to do things that we are not willing to do. We have to come up short with that, if we have really raised our children to put the Lord first then He needs to be first in all areas. We had given them over to the Lord, but it seems it was so much easier to tell others than to put that into operation ourselves. She later married John and finally got her degree at age fifty three.

Our son Dan went to a year of Bible school and then went on to graduate from U.C.L.A., and married one of the facultie's daughters. They married one weekend before our next big move, and following the Lord's leading again. I need to share with you that we were invited to the Congress of World Evangelism in Switzerland and that was an incredible time in my walk with the Lord. Earl was invited to be a representative at that congress. We had a very dear friend Paul Little who was on that committee, and he had come by our home after having a meeting with Billy Graham at a nearby hotel and asked us if we would send in our reservation. Earl said no, that we can't do something like that but Paul said that he thought we should be there. The next week when the board met for a meeting, Earl mentioned it to the board and they said 'We think you should go too and we will pay your way". There was never any discussion about my going because as I've said before we were living by faith, we had enough money to meet all our needs and God well supplied for all of those needs but we didn't have any money in the bank. Even if we would have had any money in the bank, we didn't have freedom in our own spirits to spend it for something like going overseas.

In the meantime I was working with all the programs and doing all the things I did on a weekly basis. I had a Bible study for high school girls and usually had a lady by the name of Alice Johnson that worked with me. On one particular Monday night she was not there, but called to find out how the meeting went. I told her and then went on to say that Earl wanted me to go with him to Switzerland. She mentioned at this point that she had been praying about my going with Earl to Switzerland (she had never mentioned that to me) and said that she had not only been praying for this but that she would like to give me the money to go. I had just been praying that same afternoon and told the Lord that I needed to have some kind of special sign from Him as to what He wanted us to do. To have the answer on that very night was like OH MY GOODNESS!!

That trip was really a significant time for us. We were really exposed as to what was going on in the world. There were four thousand invited guests from all over the world and we saw the tremendous things that were happening because missionaries had gone out to serve the Lord in that capacity. In the meantime, Kevin Dyer the president of International Teams had called and said "I hear you're going to go to the Congress of World Evangelism. While you are there would you consider visiting our teams in Europe and encourage them?" We said ok, that we would do that , so they bought us Euro passes and we traveled to all the different teams in Europe and had a wonderful time for three weeks visiting , seeing what they were doing, taking them all to dinner and having a great time of fellowship with them. We could see that there was a tremendous need for this.

When we flew back from Switzerland we had a layover in Chicago and who was at the airport at 2:00 am but Kevin Dyer of International Teams along with our dear friends Kay and Gary Thompson who were also with International Teams. We gave a report to them and said that we really felt that there was a great need for someone to do just what we had done in encouraging the young people that were out on the mission field. Kevin said he had been praying that we would accept that position. I was not part of that conversation, I had stepped away to talk with Kay. When we got on the plane Earl said "Do you know what Kevin asked me to do? He wants me to pray about coming to work with International Teams" Up to that point we had not been considering any change to our ministry at all. My answer was "There's no way I'm going to be leaving Culver City, we have such a fulfilling ministry where we are." Well it took two years and I just want to share the difference in making that decision. When we made the first decision I was not there spiritually. Earl was getting all kinds of direction from God's word and I didn't want to hear anything about it, which was a very stressful time. This time making this decision was not stressful. It was both of us seeking what God wanted for us and being willing to leave.

It was still a difficult time because although our daughter was now married and moving to Oregon, and Dan was getting married so we were free from raising our kids and getting them on their feet, but my mother and father were now getting elderly. One weekend we were visiting them and my husband was speaking at the church. My mother and I stayed home and talked about what her physical problems were. She just seemed more emotional than physical. I asked if it was because we were considering leaving and that is really difficult for you? She started to cry and said I wouldn't want to hold you back, I want you to do what God would have you to do and I wouldn't want to stand in the way of that. I felt I needed to assure her that we would be there whenever we were needed. Kevin had always assured me that we could always leave and be with my parents whenever they needed us, whatever amount of time that takes. So again that was the faithfulness of God, and was one of those places again to step out and trust God to meet those needs when I acted in obedience to Him. He more than provided!

Leaving Culver was a very sad thing. We had been in the Southern California area for 21 years and had many good friends and had started a new church. We shared much of our life with our wonderful friends but now it was time to follow the Lord and move on. Our last night, the church had a farewell service for us. My mother and Dad came as well as some of our friends from the Claremont area. It was hard leaving so many friends and the wonderful experiences we'd had but we knew that God was moving us and every phase of that night stands out in my memory bank of following the Lord and His faithfulness to us.

We had movers come to move us and then we drove back to Illinois. During this trip we were filled with many, many tears from leaving everyone. We soon realized that we couldn't go on that way so we stopped at a little motel and prayed for God's peace about this move. The peace that He gave us was unbelievable! We dried our eyes, went across the street to listen to a little band concert and when we got in the car to resume our trip our hearts were full of joy. Not that we never looked back, but from that time on we looked back with fond, fond memories of how God had used us and blessed us in Southern California. Now that ends our summer season.

*Fall, Season #3*, a whole new phase of life!!! Fall is one of my favorite seasons with all the different colors. We are now free to serve the Lord without the commitment to our families and caring for them.

When we got to International Teams, we moved into a house (they had homes on the grounds). They had a large administration building, a lot of other buildings, along with houses where the different teams that were training to go overseas would live. All the teams lived in these houses. You would have the French team, the Spanish team and all the teams in different houses. At this time they started a one year Bible school because this was during the '70's and there were a lot of kids coming to Christ and they were not necessarily fitting into the traditional churches. In our first year we had eight young people, guys and girls in our house. We had a large home with four bedrooms upstairs and three bedrooms in the basement and one on the first floor. This was a very adequate home for a lot of young people. The young people we had came from Canada, and several from the states. We had four girls and four guys and it was a very interesting year.

I remember the first time going to the organization meeting and finding out what my responsibilities were going to be and thinking 'oh no I don't want to do this'. I had the responsibility of making up menu's, taking care of the finances, doing the grocery shopping for the group , and had to do the cooking then be there as their counselor because Earl was teaching and so it was a very overwhelming time. I remember coming back from that first meeting, walking across the field and saying "Oh Lord, I don't think I can do this", and you know it was like the Lord saying "Oh yes, you can do it, you can be organized." Let me tell you, you have to be organized when you are cooking for that many. And then........I can remember that I had not spent a great deal of time in the kitchen , whenever we raised our kids I cooked but did not spend hours cooking and now, all of a sudden I'm spending hours in the kitchen, cooking three meals a day for all of these kids. I remember standing in the kitchen one day saying 'I hate this! This isn't something I want to do with my life Lord". Then the Lord seemed to speak to me and said "Yes, I've called you to do this and I want you to do it with a heart full of joy" Well, as I was having my quiet time that morning the Lord gave me some scriptures about a joyful heart, and doing all things for His glory, so I said ok Lord, I will praise you and I will thank you although this is not where my heart is. You will not believe this but it wasn't five minutes after I had gone back into the kitchen that I wasn't praising Him and thanking Him but I said ok, now I have to do something about this. I went and got a praise tape and put it on while I was peeling potatoes and I just started to sing and God really changed my heart.

During those years we had first ten than twelve students living with us and some were a little harder to love than others, but God showed me that I didn't have a choice, I had to love them, and He would give me the love for them. So that was our ministry there, and while we were there I also got involved in community Bible study and got into leadership as well. I did color analysis as well and that opened up a tremendous door where I started speaking at conferences and that kind of thing. I look back and I would have never said in a million years that I could have done many of those things, but when you yield yourself to the Father, He will equip you to do whatever He has called you to do.

In the summer we would take the teams overseas. We took the summer teams to Bolivia, Peru, and Ecuador, we went to Granada, St. Lucy's, St. Vincent's and that was all in our first summer. Then we would come back and get ready for more students again. Every summer we were overseas. We were in Europe quite a bit, and the time with the kids and with the missionaries was extremely profitable. We stayed with the teams, sometimes we slept in their living rooms, but had to be up at 6:30 and have the rooms straightened so that the team members could come for Bible study. We had Bible study with each one individually, took them out to dinner and counseled with them, and encouraged them. Those were just incredible years. Sometimes we would be exhausted.

I can remember one time especially that we had a team on our way to Holland. We had been with the European Missions team and had done a lot of traveling. This was when the communists were in charge of these countries. We slept in the van, and it was really not a very easy time physically. When we were on our way to Holland, I said to Earl that I was so tired that I did not think I could handle going on to another team and being ready to encourage them. Do you know when we got to the place where our team met us they said "Guess what, the house is full but we got a hotel room for you" What an answer to prayer that was! God really met that need. We took showers and just dived into bed. The next day the team called around noon to ask if we were up and we said "actually no, you just woke us up we had been so exhausted."

We spent one summer in the Philippines and that was a very interesting time. God just blessed us so much in those years that we were with the International Teams. Earl was able to develop the program for I.T. We had a lot of teachers that came from overseas and that was extremely interesting. We did that for ten years. We also had teams live with us part of that time. During this time the houses that they provided for us to live in were just beautiful and such a provision from God. We hadn't owned a home since 1965, but God provided for us so abundantly and has given us such meaningful experiences. The last house we were in was so beautiful and we used it as a hospitality house, we had people staying with us from all over. From Canada, Spain, Australia, New Zealand and so it was very enlightening and just a great opportunity for us to get to know people from other cultures.

These are just some of the things that impacted my life at this time and my love for the Lord Jesus really grew.

During these years we also had the blessed privilege of having three grandchildren born to our daughter and son-in-law in Oregon. Julie, Jessie and Jane and we were able to be at each one of their births and had many trips to Oregon to be with them. In the meantime this was a time that the health of my parents was not so good and during one of the visits back to be with them I was getting ready to go on up to Oregon but my mother looked so bad that I really felt I should not be going. She told me to go on, that I needed to be with my family and all of her needs would be taken care of but she did not want me to miss the time with my children. What a wonderful gift that was. My mother was not a woman that was real selfish and didn't say that "you need to be here with me" as a lot of other mothers would have done but instead she said to go and enjoy this time with my children. She said she had enjoyed her time with her children and now it was my time to enjoy my children.

We had promised International Teams that we would stay for ten years and we had. It was not an easy job because we were on the move so much. By this time Earl was sixty-two and we just decided it was time to retire from that kind of a ministry but we didn't know what we would do. After we had told Kevin that this was in our plans, we got a phone call from a church in Portland, Oregon. They said 'We have been thinking that you promised I.T. that you would be there for ten years and your ten years are up. How would you like to come and interview for working with us at Laurel Park?" We decided that yes maybe that is the place God would have us go. We knew a lot of people but more importantly our grandchildren were there, and our son and daughter were there. It was tremendous draw to be by our children. What a gift from God! So Earl became pastor of the church and I became involved in the church as well.

Again, it was difficult to move from Illinois, we had lots and lots of friends there and great memories. The people in the community Bible study were so kind. As I had mentioned before that we had not owned a home since 1965 and had no means to get into a home after our move to Oregon but the Lord provided for us to have a down payment to buy a house when we got to Oregon. It was absolutely a miracle that we were able to buy a home. How God has provided and His faithfulness as you trace through this story of the journey of my life, you will see that He provides more than we could ever ask or think. We lived in the Portland area for five years and it was just a delight being with our grandchildren and being very involved with them. At this point my mother and dad could come up and spend time with us as well.

By this time Earl was sixty seven and we felt it was time to retire, but had no idea how we would ever get to retire. Earl had social security but I didn't so we had to say 'ok Lord, we don't know what we're going to do but we will trust you for that'. In the meantime, our son had moved to California and I went down to be with them because we had a new little grandchild. During this time Earl got a phone call from Rawhide Boys Ranch, in Wisconsin from John Gillespie who said 'We were just wondering if you would like to come back here for an interview with us to be the director of the boys' home." Earl said "Do you realize how old I am?" But John said "That's alright, we appreciate age".

So, we thought that this was of God and here we go again, back to the mid west. That was a radical change for us. Out in the country, and in the mid west. We lived twenty minutes from the closest town. It was a beautiful ranch and it was a ministry to kids that had been placed there by the law. When we got there they had about forty boys and four homes, and by the time we left they had about sixty boys at the ranch and six homes, and we were responsible for hiring and training all the people that worked in the homes. Earl was the administrator for that and guess what.... I was his assistant!

That was the first time that I was involved in his work world and it wasn't an easy time for either of us but we made it through that first year. I was given a lot of responsibilities and this was the first time that I had a salary! I was able to be there and be an encouragement to the housemothers. I hired the cooks and did a lot of other things that I was hired to do besides being 'Earl's assistant'. I was asked to be over the kitchen crew .They prepared meals for people that came to auctions as they had a used car dealership there which was like a donation thing and when people would come to that we fed all of these people. I also had the opportunity to help put together the new homes. Buying the furniture, selecting the carpeting, and all the things that go into a new home and it was a huge job.

While we were there, we saw God do mighty works in the lives of these boys that stayed at Rawhide. During that time we were involved in a wonderful church in Appleton called Christ, the Rock. I had the opportunity to mentor and be involved with some women that were just some outstanding women in the church that had a real love for the Lord Jesus and were very gifted when it came to leadership roles. I just really came to love these women incredibly.

Those were very delightful, growing years, good years, and hard times. We had many, many difficult things to deal with, but this was God's way of providing for some of our 'winter months'. They built us a beautiful home, a four bedroom home with four bathrooms, and a great room with a huge fireplace which was just wonderful. It was also used as a hospitality house as well, and we had many guests that stayed with us. We had very long days at Rawhide but very rewarding. We really enjoyed the people and the ministry there.

When we came to Rawhide we had told them that we would come for five years and it was now six and one half years and my husband was now seventy three and the work was getting very stressful so we felt it was time for us to really retire. But where?

### *Winter, Season #4*

Our son had been looking for a place for us and found Rossmoor, in Northern California. He felt this might be a place where we could afford to live. We came to California in July and put a down payment on a two bedroom, one bath apartment that was really adequate for our needs.

As we said our goodbyes to many good people in Wisconsin, we found out that the goodbye's don't get any easier.

So, we started our winter season and had to make some more adjustments. We've been in our winter season for nine years and it has been a wonderful time here as well. The Lord opened a door for us to be involved in a Bible study at Rossmoor and Earl has been the teaching leader, and I am a discussion leader. We've about doubled in size, and we now have about eighty people in the class. We've never been involved with our contemporaries before, we're kind of the younger people here and enjoying every minute of what God has provided for us during this 'winter time of our lives'. Again I must say that God has been faithful above all that we could ask or think.

# MY STORY..... BOBBIE GARLAND

It is one of disappointment, pain and sorrow, and how God uses all circumstances to work all things together for good. Rom.8:28

Howard and I were married July 26-1946 and 10 years later I was wondering if' "this" was all there was to marriage? We had five children, endless bills, and no time for each other. My husband was a self-focused man, with a zest for living, having fun, but thinking of his pleasure first. He was exciting, good looking, and fun to be with, but those first years were very difficult as I was always at home with the kids while he went motorcycling, or on long hunting trips. I struggled with my feelings for I knew God was not pleased with my discontent, I loved my husband but felt he was not being fair to me, and I simply wanted to walk away! We were both Christians and I knew that what I wanted was wrong, but I could not or did not release it to God and ask for His guidance. We went to church Sunday, and the teacher was saying 'I believe there's someone here that is thinking of making a decision that will change their life forever, and please think of the alternative, it could be a lot worse than your circumstances are now.' I knew the Lord had sent me a message, and I knew I must listen, and obey. I had two friends that had left their husbands and their lives were total tragedies. Not once had I considered what my life might become if I left. I thanked God that He loved me so much that even in my rebellion He gave me the choice of which way I would go. I knew the scripture Malachi 2:15&16 said that God hated divorce, but I had closed my heart to His Word. I allowed Satan to blind me because of a selfish desire. I started thanking Him for my husband, who was a good man that worked hard providing for his family. The children were older and we started going on camping trips, Disney land etc. Our relationship improved, but there were still many issues to be resolved. I prayed faithfully that our marriage would be a success, and with God's help I would do all I could to make it happen. The years passed quickly, our three older children graduated, married, and had families of their own. Our two youngest boys were still at home, fourteen and nine years old when I was so weary all the time, no energy to do the daily chores, every thing was an effort. I had a lot of advice to help me feel better, but it only made me more frustrated. I had been this way for months, and felt hopeless. I was so discouraged I did not want to get out of bed. The boys were playing outside, and I was sitting in the rocking chair when they came in asking me to make them grilled cheese sandwiches. I wanted to tell them no, I cannot! Please do not ask me to do anything! But I made them and when they went outside I cried out to God 'please reveal what is wrong with me, or take me home, I don't want to live like this'! the next morning the inside of my mouth was sore so I went to the Dr. and he said there was nothing to worry about as I had an extra bone in the roof of my mouth, as many people did. He kept looking into my left eye and made an appointment with a specialist. The specialist ran a number of tests and told me I had a tumor, and sent me to a neurologist. Going to a neurologist is frightening and I was terrified. He told me I had a brain tumor, it was operable, but I would have a dry eye on the left side due to nerves being cut destroying the blinking process. I might be paralyzed on the left side, and could lose the use of my left hand. I was stunned and silently cried out to God to help me. Howard and I did not speak on the way home, we were both in shock. I had a waiting period before the operation and I walked and talked with my Savior trying to understand, and asking for faith to trust Him. 1 was frightened and was seeking for assurance and peace. 1 was reading the bible one day and 1ˢᵗ John 4:18 'Perfect love casts out fear,' seemed to be in large letters. 1 held the bible looking at those words and thinking 'but Lord my love for you is far from perfect,' so how can 1 ever have peace? The next day 1 was thinking about 'perfect love' and the Lord opened my mind to the truth of the words 'perfect love'. 1 was alone but said aloud, 'Jesus is perfect love'! 1 prayed that He would cast away my fears and He did, from that moment the fears were gone. I had no idea what was in my future but 1 knew He would be with me. Howard and 1 were in my room the night before surgery, and I asked him if he was scared and he said, yes, but 'only God can make a tree,' meaning it was all in God's hands and through the years we spoke those words to each other many times. He left and I looked at the stars and prayed Lord I will be with you tomorrow or back with my family, and may your will be done, and went to sleep trusting Him. 1 went to surgery the next morning and thirteen people walked me to the door of the operating room. I praised God for a loving and concerned family. They could not go with me any farther but by faith I reached out my hand to my Savior and He was with me through the whole procedure. I was in the hospital for three weeks. The day 1 looked in the mirror was one of the most difficult days of my life! The left side of my face was an inch lower than my right side my left eye drooped, my mouth was pulled to the left, the back of my head was shaved and I was very thin 1 cried to the Lord, why? why? He did not tell me why, and never has, but as time passed, I learned that He brings good from the painful times in a Christians life. Romans 8:28. I did not have all the results from surgery that had been a possibility and I felt better physically after surgery as the pressure was gone which would have destroyed me mentally, but 1 had a hard time dealing with the changes in my life, and appearance. I did not want to go anywhere, but my husband insisted I go with him to a restaurant that had home made pie. He knew my weakness! When 1 ate, food would drip out the left side of my mouth and 1 would not know due to the paralysis. He would reach over and wipe my face and when I looked up, embarrassed beyond words he smiled and kept talking as if it never happened. He became my caregiver, my best friend, my confidant, my helper .One day when I was alone I looked in the mirror and was crying when he came home from work early and wanted to know what was wrong. My left eye was sewn down as it was ulcerated due to lack of moisture. I cried,' just look at me I'm a candidate for a freak show'! He held me, and said 'you are more beautiful to me now than you have ever been.' Those were healing words to my emotionally scarred heart, and there as he held me I knew that God had answered my prayer for our marriage, and 1 gave Him all the glory for 'only God can make a tree.' My eye was opened after 9 months and 1 put drops in it to prevent ulceration, and still do. We had problems but trusted God to guide and direct us. My husband devoted his time and effort to help me regain my health, and 1 prayed that God would help me never to take advantage of his willing heart. 1 loved his zest for living and did not want to stifle that free spirit that had attracted me to him. The Lord was refining both our characters and teaching us to love and respect the -desires and needs of each other. Our life was good enjoying our family, friends, and-each other when a shock hit us. Our oldest son at home was meeting with other church boys and smoking pot. We could not believe it, but it was very true as he Was Caught With it at school and taken to juvenile hall. That was the beginning of a long term nightmare. Our house was suddenly filled with anger and hostility, towards him, and each other. I knew a number of couples that were separated or divorced, due to their children using drugs, and 1 did not want disagreements over how to discipline our son to come between us. His drug habit escalated from marijuana to hard drugs, and our home was literally a battle field. 1 started praying that God would help us keep our marriage a priority, and not let Satan use drugs to destroy us. It was very hard to deal with a son under the influence of narcotics as a mother's desire is to save and protect that son from all harm, and all he thought about was how to use us to get another fix. There was turmoil and arguments constantly and 1 knew the tensions between us had to be resolved or our marriage would be in serious trouble. 1 prayed constantly that God would help us know how to keep our relationship strong, and it was very simple as He caused both of us to realize we had to respect the other one's ideas. Our son would not listen to us so we gave our support to each other and prayed for him. We never gave up on him, praying that he would come to his senses and turn away from that life. Our youngest son started to Jr. High and his life of drugs. It is hard to describe the pain and fear that becomes your daily life when your children become addicts. The telephone ringing in the middle of the night frightens you, the sound of sirens leaves you weak and shaking. Trips to the hospital praying he is alive, rescuing from jail praying he has learned his lesson. My husband was more realistic than I was and said we had to stop, that we could not continue rescuing them. To a certain extent we did, but there was times we rushed to the hospital expecting our youngest son to be dead. Many nights I would lie awake until I heard him come in and, would be very tired the next day. 1 prayed the Lord would help me sleep, and He did! I would not even hear him when he came home which I called a miracle!! Due to drugs our youngest son had a gun accident and lost his right leg, which compounded our problems. He tried living alone two different times but was unable to do it, so he came back home. He was very resourceful and after rehab was able to care for his personal needs. We both met all the other needs that a paralyzed person has. It was another challenge and we worked together praying for his recovery. God gave us the grace to help our son and to care for him 'as unto the Lord. '1 remembered how gracious God was to stop me from a big mistake many years ago, and because He did we were facing a difficult situation together. How thankful I was that my husband was right beside me and 1 often thought what would I do without him? 1 cannot put into words the pain, disappointments, fears and tensions drugs cause. The trembling at the sound of a siren, the heart pounding at late night telephone calls, the weakness when there is pounding on the door at an early morning hour, going from door to window looking down the road when they don't come home is all part of the agony of addiction. The Lord taught me to trust Him and place our boys on the altar, and leave them there for Him to work in their lives. It was hard but I knew 1 must step aside and not hinder what God wanted to do. It is never a one time commitment, but a decision I am still making with God's help. Our older son married and gave his heart to the Lord and lives a normal life blessing our lives as we saw the remarkable change that only God could do.

The younger son stayed with us, and we accepted that he would continue taking drugs and although we did not like his life style he needed us and we did all we could to help him. He was making all the wrong choices and we had to stand by and watch him suffer the consequences, and he truly did. He is in a power chair and only has the use of his left arm and hand, due to another accident. Those were difficult years but we prayed that God would give us a double portion of His grace to meet the problems and.serve Him as we ministered to our son. It was not always as simple as saying 'we trust God.' We felt like giving up many times, but we remembered that Jesus never gave up walking to the cross and never gives up on us.

A number of years went by and one day I lost the use of my left leg, I could not walk without help from my husband. We went to the Dr. and after many tests they admitted they did not know what caused the loss. I had regained the use of my leg after a few days, but they told me I had a cyst in my entire spinal column. I could have surgery with three shunts to drain the fluid and they did not know if my spine would collapse when the fluid was removed. The Dr. said it was a 50-50 chance of paralysis either way. Again, we were stunned, and could not give the Dr. an answer. We prayed for God's guidance and asked for wisdom for ourselves and for the Dr. My husband left the final decision up to me, and after much prayer I decided not to have the operation and trust the Lord to help me whatever happened. Many years later I am still walking with a walker and the Dr. says the cyst has done all the damage it will do. My mobility is impaired but I walk very deliberate and slow, praising God for each step. One of our daughters had an exploratory surgery and stage 4 ovarian cancer was discovered throughout her abdomen. We felt over whelmed and pled with God in prayer to save her life. She has had many surgeries since and suffered deeply, but is now cancer free, praise God!

We learned many valuable lessons through those experiences that prepared us for a greater sorrow. After my 70th birth day I had a major heart attack, a hip replacement and my husband was called home to be with the Lord. A few months later my other hip broke, and last year I had a fractured back. My son is still living with me, and still struggles with his addiction, but is much better. He goes to re-habilitation in two weeks, which gives him a chance to clear his head and hope fully start a new life.

My other daughter had breast cancer and after three surgeries and 6 weeks of radiation she is also cancer free. The news left me asking why would both my daughters have cancer? God always has His purpose, and many good things came about because of it, and I learned once again to trust my Heavenly Father because He does all things well, even when it hurts!

My husband was right beside me through my heart attack, and the hip replacement. He was a wonderful caregiver. I could not lift or bend so he did it for me and helped with all the house work. He drove me every where putting my walker in and out of the car, attending to my every need. My heart overflowed with gratitude to my Heavenly Father for the treasure He knew would be mine when He stopped me years ago and I love Him for the wonderful gift of a loving husband.

My greatest loss was when my husband went home to be with the Lord, I did not think I could live through it, I blamed God, could not understand why He took him from me. I was in so much pain I cried out to God 'you made us one and now you have tom us apart, how can I go on with out him'? I wrote out my feelings, and then put God's answer to them from His word and have included them as they convey the struggle I had. I have repented many times for the way I felt that God had betrayed me, but praise Him He understands our grief and grieves with us. I was reading Psalm 23 and when I read 'He restoreth my soul,' I prayed this prayer:" Lord, I know my soul is secure in You, but this past year it has been deeply wounded with an unbearable sorrow I know this great loss is because we live in a fallen world.· So

Lord, I am asking You to restore my wounded soul. As You promised in Psa.23.Each morning I quote "The joy of the Lord my strength" but I feel very little joy .I need You to restore the joy that only You can give. I thank You for Your love, mercy and grace through this difficult time, even if I do not feel it. I believe Your promises, but admit that sorrow has overshadowed them, but I am trusting You to bring me to full restoration."

I am taking care of my son, our home and all the responsibilities and truly 'only God can make a tree,' as 1 did not think 1 could do what 1 am now doing; it is only by God's strength and grace. One of my favorite verses is 11 Chronicles 16:9a 'For the eyes of the Lord run to and fro throughout the whole earth, to show Him self strong on behalf of those whose heart is loyal to Him.' Whatever my future holds 1 will be loyal to Him, and He will never leave me or forsake me. My husband's health declined for two months and 1 wrote my feelings down as the disease progressed which explains the depth of my sorrow.

My last question 'will there be a brighter to marrow?' Yes, but it did take time and many tears, but God has been faithful and met my needs. 1 will always miss my husband but 1 have the wonderful promise that 1 will see him again and we will worship our Lord together. Many years ago 1 was feeling sorry for myself and told my husband 'Nobody likes me,' and he held my hand and said 'I do.' One week after his death 1 was crying and saying 'no one will ever love me like he did.' 1 felt God's presence, and heard Him say 'I do,' and 1 have found that to be true these last three years. 1 have remembered those words "I do" many times and relied on that love and it has never failed.

## Feelings vs Fact

Like an orphan                    Your Father
11 Cor. 6: 18 I will be a Father unto you, and ye shall be my sons and daughters.

So alone and lonely               Your Companion
Heb. 13:5 I will never leave thee or forsake thee.

Like crying all the time          Your Consolation
Rev.21:4 God shall wipe away all tears from their eyes; and there shall be no more death, neither sorrow, nor crying, neither shall there be any more pain.

Like my heart is broken           Your Healer
Isaiah 61: 1-2 He hath sent me to bind up the broken hearted; and to comfort all that mourn.

So confused and troubled          Your Peace
John 14:27 Peace I leave with you, my peace I give unto you; let not your heart be troubled, neither let it be afraid.

Inadequate to the task            Your Counselor
Psalms 73:24 Thou shalt guide me with Thy counsel, and afterward receive me into glory.

Overwhelmed                       Your Sufficiency
11 Cor.3:5 not that we are sufficient of ourselves to think anything as of ourselves; but our sufficiency is of God.

Disconnected from life            Your Life
Acts 17:.28 In Him we live, and move. and have our being; we are His offspring.

So helpless                       Your Helper
Psalms 46: 1 God is our refuge and strength, a very present help in trouble.

So weak and frail             Your Strength
Isaiah 41: 10 Fear thou not, for I am with thee, be not dismayed~ for I am thy God, I will strengthen thee~ yea I will help. thee; yea I will uphold thee with the right hand of my righteousness.

So weary and restless         Your Rest
Matt. 11: 28 Come unto me, all ye that labor and are heavy laden, and I will give you rest.

So sad and fearful            Your Comforter
Isaiah 51: 12 I, even I am He that comforteth you; who art thou that thou shouldst be afraid.

So abandoned and alone      Your Best Friend
Isaiah 49: 16 I have graven thee upon the palms of my hands; thy walls are ever before me (or always in my memory.) Isaiah 41: 13 For I the Lord thy God, will hold thy right hand, saying unto thee, fear not; I will help thee.

So insecure.                  Your Security
Romans 8: 38-39 For **I** am persuaded that neither death, nor life, nor angels, nor principalities, nor powers, nor things present, nor things to come, nor height, nor depth, nor any other creature, shall be able to separate us from the love of God, which is in Christ Jesus our Lord.

So incomplete              Your Fulfillment
Col. 2: 10 You are complete in Him, who is the head of all principality and power (niv). You have been given

fullness in Christ, who is the head over every power and authority.

So betrayed                              Your Surety
Jer. 29: 11 For I know the thoughts that I think towards you, says the Lord, thoughts of peace and not of evil, to give you a future and a hope.

Num. 23: 19 God is not a man that He should lie, nor a son of man, that He should repent. Has He said, and will He not do? Or has He spoken, and will He not make it good?

## My Lament

*Lord, I love him so,*
*Does he really have to go?*
*I want your will, I do*
*But regardless, I want him too.*
*Lord, can't you see how lonely I'll be?*
*And how I need him close to me!*
*He's my very best friend*
*Is this friendship soon to end?*
*I went to prayer today*
*But I didn't even know how to pray*
*Lord I'm so confused and mixed up,*
*Must I accept this sorrow filled cup?*
*Last night he struggled for air*
*I'm sorry Lord, but this just isn't fair!*
*Today, in his eyes I saw tears*
*Is he struggling with unknown fears?*
*He went to church today,*
*He didn't comprehend, he worshipped, he*
    *prayed.*
*He's waiting on death row*
*Please heal him, you can; I know.*

*Why are people laughing, having fun?*
*All I feel is darkness, no light, no sun.*
*Paula brought us a beautiful flower,*
*An Easter lily; symbol of resurrection*
*power.*
*Easter Sunday; it's the day I met You,*
*One year later, he met You, too.*
*My heart is heavy and sad,*
*I so want him to live; is that so bad?*
*Kathryn brought a video of cheer*
*She is thoughtful, kind, and dear.*
*Chemo is Tuesday, and I dread it so,*
*Will he be sick? I wonder, but I don't*
*know.*
*Cancer, chemo, doctors! Why Lord? I*
*don't understand.*
*But I do know; his name is written in Your*
*hand!*
*Laquita came to help, and her love to*
*share*
*Cooking, cleaning, she proved how much*
*she cared.*
*Hold him close, comfort and sustain him*
*Prepare his heart as his life dims.*
*Sherry came with a pot of stew.*
*I love your children Lord, they remind me*
*of you.*
*Linda came to be with her Dad*
*Their moments were special, tender, but*
*sad.*
*Lord, who is going to put my shoes on,*
*Carry out trash, gas the car, who? When*
*I'm alone?*
*Eileen came with muffins, cookies and*
*bread*
*Giving support, just as Your Word says.*

*He had his first chemo today*
*He didn't get sick, because of You, he did*
    *okay.*
*Ruth came smiling, with a complete meal*
*Her heart so tender, her love so real.*
*It's hard for him to breathe enough air,*
*Lord, please help him; I know you care!*
*Geoff hugged him, crying, loving him so*
*"You are a good dad," he wanted him to*
    *know.*
*After chemo he was so weak, Geoff*
    *sobbed, holding him tight*
*Thank you Lord, it was a beautiful sight.*
*He's so tired, confused, and very weak.*
*Strengthen him Lord, your mercy I seek.*
*Lord as the time draws near*
*Must you take one, so dear?*
*In bed we hold hands, and our feet touch*
*You can see Lord, we love each other so*
    *much.*
*Ratha and Pete came to help and be near,*
*Working side by side, watching, praying*
    *for their friend so dear.*
*When Howie came, he smiled with delight,*
*Father and son, hugging, for a moment all*
    *was right.*
*I'm hurting Lord, but I submit to your will,*
*With a heart of sadness; Lord it's how I*
    *feel.*
*I know it's almost time for him to leave,*
*Hold me close, comfort me, as I weep and*
    *grieve.*
*When Geoff crawled into his room, crying,*
    *"Dad, I love you",*
*My heart shattered, without him, Lord!*
    *What will we do?*

*Kathryn and Paula were special through it*
*all*
*Driving, bringing food, ready to help, at*
*my call.*
*He was sleeping when your angels came*
*To take him home, when you called his*
*name.*
*I know he's now with you, enjoying*
*heaven's bliss,*
*But his smile, his tender look, his touch, I*
*already miss.*
*So Lord bear with me through this time of*
*sorrow*
*Longing for him; I wonder, will there be a*
*brighter tomorrow?*

----------------------

# MY STORY....SHEILA COLCLASURE

CANCER. Non-Hodgkins Lymphoma. What? What had the doctor said? My husband, Larry, and I sat there in total shock and disbelief.

> ...But God proved Himself faithful, as He always had,
> Let me start at the beginning...

When I was 5 years old we started a church in our house. Our family had moved from Arkansas to Santa Ana, California and the church was actually started in our little house on 1st street. As a little girl, I remember sitting under the keyboard of the piano during services. I accepted Christ at the age of 7 in the bathroom of our house while sitting on my Mom's lap! Even as a little girl I loved being involved in church services and music.

Larry and I met at that same church in California in 1969, when he came to apply for the part-time choir director position. (He was in the Marine Corps at the time.) I was the church organist. One Sunday he walked up to the organ, looked into my eyes and fell in love with me!! It took me a bit longer however. But not by very much! I was engaged at that time to the man who later married my sister. It didn't take me long to realize that Larry Colclasure was the one for me. We met in February, were engaged in April and married in June. I knew a good thing when I saw it.

We had been married for four months when the Military transferred us to Hawaii. This was when the Vietnam War was at its hottest and most volatile – and yet God chose to send us to the beautiful island of Oahu. It was there we attended International Baptist Church pastored by Dr. James R. Cook. I was very privileged to work as Dr. Cook's secretary for the two years that we lived in Hawaii. In the years to come, Larry would struggle with survivor's guilt as he would be reminded of the many men and women who had lost their lives fighting in that far away country while he was stationed in Hawaii. And then one day God whispered to him in prayer; "I could have sent you anywhere and brought you home safely. But I sent you and Sheila to Hawaii to be under Pastor Jim's ministry." It was under his ministry that a very firm foundation was laid for our marriage. Had it not been for those two years of mentoring from Pastor Jim, I'm not sure our marriage would have survived the later years.

Larry was honorably discharged from the military and we moved back to California where we lived until 1973. We then moved (along with our year old son) to Lynchburg, Virginia where Larry enrolled as a student in what is now Liberty University. He graduated in 1976, and the next year we added another little boy to our family. For six years Larry worked on the youth staff at Thomas Road Baptist Church. We grew to love hundreds of kids' as we became involved in their lives. A great number of those "kids" are serving in full-time ministry around the world today. We are humbled as we think back on what an awesome privilege God allowed us during those years.

In 1980, we moved to Dallas and Larry became part of the staff at a local church. It was while serving there that Larry started dealing with issues in his life that brought about crisis and a dark time for us. In 1987, he admitted to me that he was struggling with what we would later learn was sexual addiction. I was in total shock and despair! I thought I had married the 'perfect man' and that image had been shattered. Larry resigned from the church and we went into combat.

We struggled financially for what seemed like an eternity. He would pick up odd jobs wherever he could, but it was very hard. There were times I couldn't buy certain groceries in order to buy the boy's socks or underwear. However, we were never late on our house payment and the utilities were always paid on time. Amazingly, there were even times money would just appear in our mailbox

During the darkness, God became very real in my life – Larry's as well. I vividly remember taking countless showers because it was the safest place to cry my heart out without the boys hearing me. I could sense God's presence in my aloneness there. It was like God showing up in the fiery furnace with the Hebrew children. I could hear Him whispering to me, "You better stay with this guy. I'm going to take you places that you're not going to believe." This conversation happened over and over. So, I decided to walk the journey with them – Larry and God. The uncertain journey was as painful as it was terrifying. Journal entries from those lonely days in the desert reflect my deepest struggles: "Did I really love him?" "Could I stay with him?" "Could I ever trust him again?" and "What was best for the boys?".

Through many hours of counseling, prayer and the decision to stay, the healing process began. I'll never forget the day my counselor walked me to my car, put his arm around my shoulder and said, "Sheila, you're going to have a life someday." Oh, how I wanted to believe that.

So I hung tightly to God - and to Larry - while working on some of my own issues. And God has indeed done "exceeding abundantly above all that I could ask or think"!

Today Larry is a therapist in private practice. We minister to dozens of men who are struggling with this ever-increasing disease. The Internet is a wonderful tool in the right hands, but it has become a devastating tool in the hands of others. Larry's practice mainly consists of wonderful, godly men who have become ensnared in this seemingly harmless "secret sin". There are many ways sexual addiction manifests itself, the results always devastating. It is our joy to see God restore families and marriages. We are so blessed to have a ministry to hurting people. People just like us. In my wildest dreams I could not have imagined where and how God would be using us today. Would I walk that painful road again? ABSOLUTELY!! To be where we are today – I would absolutely walk that road again

During those years, our boys grew up, moved out and pursued their own dreams. I was working in Larry's office, his practice was flourishing and life was good. It had all finally come together...

Until May 2002, when I was diagnosed with Non-Hodgkins Lymphoma. I was having severe pain in my back and my doctor ordered a CSAT thinking I probably had a kidney stone. I had the CSAT on Friday and within two hours the doctor called. Larry handed the phone to me and she asked if I was having weakness in my legs. I answered that "yes and I could hardly walk". She told me she was going to admit me to the hospital immediately because I had a blood clot in my leg and then she asked to talk to Larry.

Larry listened carefully as she said: "Even though my office is already closed, I want you and Sheila to come to the back door where I will be waiting for you". Larry suspected that there was more than just a blood clot. There, she told us I probably had Non-Hodgkin's Lymphoma. It was a bolt out lightning out of the blue. I asked about my prognosis. She said, "30% chance of recovery or two years of life." More conclusive tests were needed.

It was a roller coaster of emotions. There were times I struggled with the unknown. There were days that I was very depressed, then the next day would be easier. The whole process was almost like I was living someone else's life, but each morning would bring the realization that it was, indeed, my life. I told Larry that I didn't want to die. Just being able to say those words to him was a relief to me.

While I was in the hospital we received a phone call, and that person said, "How could God let this happen? Sheila is a godly woman." To be honest, that thought had never crossed our minds. Our focus was always that God get glory from this as we walked this journey. Larry and I just wanted His will to be done. We desperately wanted me to be well, but we found great comfort in knowing that He saw the big picture. That He was working "everything for our good because we loved Him", Rom. 8:28. He promised that He would do that.

The diagnosis of Non-Hodgkins Lymphoma was confirmed. I was referred to an oncologist at a cancer treatment center. Ironically, I had driven by this very treatment center many times, always thanking God I didn't have cancer. Now we were sitting in an office at the treatment center waiting to meet MY oncologist for the very first time. God used that doctor to reassure my hope when he walked in and said, "This is treatable and curable." And time has proven him right!

In her book <u>Diamonds In The Dust</u>, Joni Eareckson Tada writes: "I Thessalonians 5:16-18 says, *"Be joyful always; pray continually; give thanks in all circumstances, for this is God's will for you in Christ Jesus."* God is not asking us to *be* thankful but to *give* thanks. There's a big difference between feeling thankful and giving thanks. One response involves emotions, the other, your will.  Trusting God has absolutely nothing to do with trustful feelings.

Also, God's not asking us to give thanks **for** the tough times – only that we give thanks **in** them.  Give thanks that He is sovereign...that He is in control...giving you grace and peace...and planning it all for your good and His glory."

The Sunday morning following my first chemo treatment, I was getting ready for church.  I reached up to fix my hair and found large clumps of hair were coming out in my hand.  That was devastating to me! How un-feminine, a bald woman.  Our oldest son, David, was visiting at the time and remarked, "Just think, Mom, every hair that falls out is a piece of the cancer coming out."  So, the next Sunday I donned my cute new wig and off to church I went!

I lost ALL of my hair.  While lying on the couch one day, totally exhausted from the poison in my system, hairless, and without make-up Larry walked in, looked at me, smiled and said, "You're so cute!"  I love that man.

I had six chemo treatments and have done beautifully since then.  My sweet husband was my rock through it all.

Larry came home from his office one afternoon and we were praying together. He prayed, "Lord, people have been so good to us, but please don't let them forget my sweet Sheila as this journey continues."  Immediately the doorbell rang and there stood a deliveryman with a beautiful bouquet of flowers sent from good friends who live in Florida.  Again, God said "I'm still in control.  I haven't forgotten you."

The support from family and friends was overwhelming.  These wonderful people more than met our needs and even our wants.  Friends held my hand as my head was shaved, flowers were planted in our flower beds and on the occasions that Larry couldn't go, there was always a sweet friend who would be there when I received treatment. Larry works late one night a week and our youngest son would come and keep me company on those long nights.

One of the most dreaded side effects from chemo is nausea. Thanks to a wonderful new medication I never experienced nausea from my treatments. My worst days were when God seemed far away. Larry reminded me of what John Eldredge (author of Wild at Heart) said at a training seminar – that when we feel like we're not hearing from God, sometimes He is really saying to us, "You know the right thing to do and I trust you to do it." God promised me that He would never leave me and I knew that, but sometimes it was necessary to do the hard thing and decide that I could trust Him, by faith, and make it through another minute, hour or day.

Today, August 2006, I have been cancer free almost four years. In fact yesterday I got another "clean" report from my oncologist. He said, "You're doing so well I really don't know what to do with you." I know my life is totally in His hands and whatever the outcome would have been;, I find great comfort in the realization that He is in control - always. He loves me beyond comprehension and desires the best for my life, battling for me. So......... I'm resting in Him. My life (and yours) is totally in His hands - and I trust Him with it.

I want to leave you with words to a song which are very special to me.

# THROUGH
## Written by Bill and Gloria Gaither

When I saw what lay before me
"Lord," I cried, "what will you do?"
I thought He would just remove it
But He gently led me through

CHORUS
Without fire, there's no refining
Without pain, no relief
Without flood, there's no rescue
Without testing, no belief

Through the fire, through the flood
Through the water, through the blood
Through the dry and barren places
Through life's dense and maddening mazes
Through the pain and through the glory
Through will always tell the story
Of a God who's power and mercy
Will not fail to take us through

Be encouraged! God will indeed see us through –
whatever our circumstances, whatever our struggle.
We are precious in His sight.

# MY STORY..... MARYLIN D. BLAIR

Joy for My Journey -- September, 2006

I just returned from helping move my 91 year old Mother into an Assisted Living center in Southern Virginia. This was a very hard journey for her, a difficult passage for my four brothers and me – her only daughter. Memories of her walk of faith filled my thoughts. I recalled how she always had time to give to others, to help others, to be concerned for their needs. From early childhood on we were raised to care, to serve God through helping others.

Like many families we are all scattered on both coasts: eldest brother in Florida, middle and youngest brothers in California, another brother in the state of Washington, and me in the Mid-Atlantic region of the East Coast. Although separated by many miles, we stay connected through reunions, phone, and email. As the years pass I realize more and more how special family is, and why God chooses to put us in earthy as well as His very own special "adopted" family.

I entered my earthy family some sixty years ago. At age nine, I recall becoming part of God's adopted family one Sunday morning. I simply "asked Jesus into my heart". That day, I felt the spirit of God tug at my heart. Ever afterwards I have sensed God's secure hold on my heart and life. In the years that followed, I certainly experienced my share of stumbles, sorrows and dark places, as well as indescribable joys that only knowing the Lord can bring.

In my life journey, I married young -- innocent, and naïve. It was always my intent to be paired with a devoted Christian. After all, hadn't I graduated from a Christian college, been active in one of the most progressive churches, had the best Sunday School teachers, and heard some of the greatest sermons? I won't go into all the details, because thirty-five years later they no longer matter. But, nothing had prepared me for the kind of misery, loneliness, and despair a failed marriage can bring. I believe there is no greater loneliness than the aloneness I experienced while married. I remembered a phrase from the book, Pilgrims Progress, where wandering meaninglessly through life was described as the "Slough of Despond". As far as I was concerned, that phrase described where I wandered for about 20 years. Of course there were many good moments in this period because of the birth of two wonderful children – my son, Phil and daughter, Christina. But, that would be their story to tell.

I vividly recall facing the discouraging truth of my situation one morning. Mine had become a life full of pain, sadness, and debt. As I looked in the bathroom mirror I felt a voice come from deep within saying, "You are going to make it". I knew this was the Holy Spirit speaking directly to me. A reassuring scripture came to mind -- a prophetic message from ages ago, "I will restore unto you the years the locusts have stolen". I held desperately to that promise! Twenty years later, I can truly say that my life has been restored many times over.

So many blessings followed my lowest spot. First, a friend from church put a substantial check in my hands saying, "I believe the Lord wants you to have this money." My bank, instead of foreclosing, let me stay in the house, pay as I was able until a year later I was fully caught up on the mortgage. I had an opportunity to join a Business Consulting firm that was increasingly successful financially. My son was accepted to and graduated from West Point. My daughter survived a stormy adolescence. Both, though bruised, are now fine adults. And, I have the extra reward of grandchildren! Oh yes, God can be counted on to keep His promises. In the book of John it says Jesus came to bring life -- an abundant, full, and overflowing life. I can only say that the life I began to experience was very full.

One would think that after hard evidence of God's goodness I would not make a dumb statement like, "I'm never going to marry again". I should have learned by now that God takes pleasure in the unexpected! He looks for ways to give us special gifts and delights. I like to think of it as serendipity – unexpected joys!

By this time I had remained single a good ten years, had a very successful consulting career, and was financially secure far beyond my wildest hopes. I was now President of my own Consulting Company, active in various Civic Organizations, Chairman of a University Business School Board, recipient of numerous awards, including recognition from the state of Maryland, winner of local and state Small Business Administration Awards – the full package. My life was good indeed. Just when you think you have it all, you find that the Lord has prepared yet another delight.

Into my busy, full and overflowing life came a wonderful friend, Dave. Our sons had been best friends all through Junior and Senior High School. We later learned that they used to joke and wonder, "wouldn't it be great if your Mom and my Dad got together

Now, both Dave and I were self-proclaimed, card carrying members of the "never going to marry again" club. Did I say earlier in this piece that God is fond of bestowing unexpected delights? Well, God is able to give you a new heart and new eyes to see things differently. Serendipity it was, and some 14 years later our fledgling friendship has evolved into a seasoned, God-sensitive, solid, tested, and loving marriage relationship.

173

Because Dave and I both put friendship first, we talked about everything and anything. Conversations lasted for hours – precious, unhurried times of trying to understand what mattered most to each. Out mutual priorities were: God first, everything else follows. Funny how placing God in first place makes all else fall where needed! Our sacred promise to each other was that we would take everything to God: choices, upsets, communications, and any misunderstandings. All had to pass the Lord's honest scrutiny before insisting on our own way. How and when the Lord leads became our "gold" standard. What the Lord was helping us slowly learn was trust. Trust first in a shared, caring God, and eventually trust that forms the bedrock faith we would need for trials ahead.

Dave and I married in June, 1992 circled and blessed by five grown children, and friends, as well as extended family. We asked each of our children if they would like to participate in our ceremony in some way. Our eldest son sang "Morning Has Broken", symbolizing new beginnings for us. Each son or daughter shared special thoughts, giving us their blessings. Two of my brothers came from the west coast to walk me down the aisle. I was reminded that Jesus' first miracle was at the wedding of friends. And, Jesus' return to gather together all those he loves and who love him is likened to a bridegroom coming for his bride. I can only imagine the looks on all our faces that glorious day when we will see all those who know and love the Lord.

I believe that all relationships are worked out in rather ordinary days and ways. What followed for Dave and I were three wonderful years of exploring, learning, and grounding in our mutual faith walk. However, we know to expect trails in this life. No exceptions! In the fall of 1995, Dave's position of 32 years at a major corporation was eliminated: He was offered and took "early retirement." We have often talked about how God knew this was ahead for us, and paved the way for us to be married and somewhat settled to cushion the blow. Dave went through a very challenging two years of refocusing his life. When a person's primary work identify is suddenly ripped away, all kinds of issues of self-worth, fairness, and questions about the future arise. Fortunately, Dave was very active in an international Bible Study group. He was surrounded by men who practiced the power of faith and prayer, who truly believed in the goodness of God. They were an awesome support system for Dave, as well as me.

Of course we experienced feelings of anger and sadness about how and when Dave was "retired", but overall we were grateful for God's provision. Dave often said that he did not know how he would have made it through without me. He valued my encouragement, practical outlook, and faith that all would turn out well. We had opportunity to practice our beliefs as expressed in the book of Romans that "all things" work out for those who love God and are called according to His purpose.

Then, nearly four years later, in the spring of 2000, I was diagnosed with breast cancer. Oddly, I was spared the fairly common question – why me? I remember a verse in the Bible that says "the rain falls on the just and the unjust". I also knew that trails are just a part of life. Because I was spared the "why me" questions that plague many who receive a cancer diagnosis, I was able to move ahead with decisions regarding treatment options. One of our dear friends, a cardiologist, referred me to the top Breast Cancer Oncologist at Johns Hopkins Hospital. Normally, I would not be able to get an appointment with her for weeks or months. She saw me that very week. In June, 2000, on our 8 year wedding anniversary, I underwent a bilateral mastectomy. Because of the severity of my diagnosis it was recommended that I follow-up with both chemotherapy and radiation.

We had a vast network of "angels" praying for me. All over the country, family and friends offered prayer support. One of my brothers held a prayer vigil for me during me entire surgery. That first night post-surgery, nurses kept asking me if I would like some pain medication. I said," no, I don't need any". I was able to get up, push my IV trolley, and return to bed unaided. Finally, around 3 am a nurse said, "are you sure you don't want any pain medication?" I replied that I did have a bit of a headache, and would like an aspirin. The nurse gave me an odd look, and said she would have to check with my Dr. since he had prescribed a much stronger painkiller! Eventually, she brought aspirin. I went home later that same day.

We had arranged for a home health nurse to stop by our house, and show Dave how to change my dressings and take care of the drainage tubes. When she came the next day, she asked for some basic medical history. One of her questions was "how is the pain?" I responded, "I have no pain". Astonished, she said "you have experienced no pain? None?" I told her that so many people had been praying for me that I felt no pain from the surgery. To this day it remains a mystery – how could I be stitched from east to west, and experience no pain? The only way I can describe my entire surgery experience was that it was like being lifted up on "angel wings". From the pre-surgery moment I began reciting the comforting words of Psalm 23 until I started chemotherapy I felt absolutely no pain! I know that it is impossible, but it happened. We truly have a God, for whom nothing is impossible.

Chemotherapy was another matter entirely. It was one six month period I definitely would not care to repeat. I believe that most people experiencing my particular chemotherapy would agree. In fact, my fellow chemo travelers referred to one concoction as "the red devil". I think that describes my experience pretty well. Dave was a marvelous support during this difficult time. In fact, at the first sign of hair loss, I asked and he shaved my head. We both cried, and just went through it together. And, Gus, our sensitive Australian shepherd would not leave my side. Any time I coughed, he would look at me as if to say, "are you alright?" To be surrounded by such love is a blessing beyond imagination. I echo Dave's words, "I don't know how I would have gone through it without you".

Our family and friends – especially our church community -- really nurtured us during this time, bringing meals, sending cards, checking in. I have never had such an outpouring of caring. Clients send flowers, books and other gifts. Friends and family sent cards and gifts. My sister-in-law sent a book entitled "Joy for the Journey." I read and re-read that book every day for a whole year. While going through one of the toughest times of my life, I experienced some of the greatest joy! I have since given copies of this book away to others going through difficult life experiences. These experiences taught me one of faith's most mysterious paradoxes, that God's strength is made perfect in our weakness. I was too weak to do anything but turn everything over to the Lord. During this time I remained as active as I could in my Bible study class. These courageous women held me in prayer constantly, and surrounded me with their love. I cannot tell you how many women and men remembered me and held me up in prayer, because I truly do not know how many. I have never experienced anything like the blessing of being held in prayer – for months. God's grace is too marvelous. I felt very humbled by this outpouring of God's spirit!

Following chemo, I began radiation treatments, which were tiring but manageable. During my first radiation treatment it dawned on me that the two staff present planned to leave the room so they would not be exposed to the radiation I would receive. I remember being a bit frightened by my aloneness. When I looked up at the ceiling of the treatment room, there above the massive equipment, the lasers used to pinpoint radiation rays formed a perfect cross. So, there I was, beneath the cross. It was a great comfort to me to be under the sign of the cross the next twenty-six times!

When I began my cancer experience – I did not know it would be an entire year of surgery, recovery and treatment. One day I found a verse in the second chapter of Song of Solomon, "See! The winter is past; the rains are over and gone. Flowers appear on the earth; the season of singing has come, the cooing of doves is heard in our land." That verse encouraged me to think about spring. I completed my last radiation treatment on the first day of Spring, 2001. How like the Lord to put a promise into your heart, then deliver on the exact day! What a wonderful God we know. I love the old hymn that talks about "joy unspeakable". My heart was full to overflowing. I have often said that going through cancer treatments, as a life experience is pretty dreadful, but as a spiritual experience I highly recommend it! I would not trade the blessings I received from the Lord for anything in this world. I adore the title of C.S. Lewis' book, "Surprised by Joy". I truly was surprised by the joy that God brings into our lives!

After completing my five years of oral cancer therapy, I have been released by my oncologist to my regular Dr. I do not know what the future holds, but I know the One who does know. And, I know His promises can be counted on -- are sure and worthy. I know the Lord has such amazing love in copious amounts, because I have experienced it firsthand. I also know that He gives love to last for a lifetime, more than I deserve. I am blessed to receive such love. I am writing this story to pass it on!

# MY STORY.....PAULINE GRANT

God has blessed my life in many, many ways.

I remember when...

I was five years old. God had given me wonderful Christian parents and I grew up knowing about Jesus, but during a Sunday evening service at our church God was tugging at my young heart and I realized that I needed to have Jesus live in *my* heart and so I invited Him in. Therefore I have no great and marvelous story about how God delivered me from a life of terrible sin, but it was the best decision I ever made and I have trusted God to lead me every day of my life.

I remember when...

It was time to venture out into the world, get my college education and prepare for my life's work. As a seventeen-year-old, that was a scary time, but God led me to Pacific Bible College (now Azusa Pacific University). There I received a good education and made many new friends including the man that God had planned for me. Isn't it amazing how God leads us in the tiniest details of our lives and many times we don't understand those until we look back on them later and realize that He had this marvelous plan for us all along. Even though that road is often bumpy and there may be detours that we don't understand, still I saw God's hand and His wonderful plan for us.

I remember when...

God provided a job at the college so I could help pay for my education. As "Assistant Dean of Students" during my senior year (big title for an ordinary student) one of my jobs was to see that all the students were in their rooms at ten o'clock before I locked the gates to the girls' patio. One night I was visiting with some girls when one of them asked me what I was going to do when I graduated and I said that I didn't know. Dr. Haggard had asked me to be *the* cook for the college but the thought of that scared the daylights out of me and I knew I couldn't do it. Well, one of the girls said, "You ought to go see my mother. She does the hiring for La Puente Schools." I told her that sounded like a great idea, but that it couldn't possibly work since I hadn't had any education courses. She assured me it didn't matter—they needed teachers desperately (it was 1953 and the schools were flooded with post-war babies). So I got up my courage, went for an interview, was invited back the next day to meet the superintendent and was hired! What a miracle! God certainly provided the impossible for me with that job. I *loved* teaching and that led ultimately to a very fulfilling career in education. After retiring from 27 years of teaching in the public school, I had the opportunity to be a Student Teacher Mentor for Azusa Pacific University for another twelve years.

I remember when...

Like most young girls, I was desperately hoping that God was preparing a wonderful young man whom I would fall in love with and who would ultimately ask me to marry him. I had been assigned to accompany a trombonist named Don Grant. That meant that we needed to practice together at a prescribed time each weekday. He lived off-campus and I lived on campus, so other than practice times we didn't see much of each other. We became good friends, but I was totally surprised when, in May, he asked me for a date. From that time on we were very good friends and today, after 53 years of marriage, he is still my very best friend. He tells people - "She was my accompanist, and I was so impressed with her accompanying that I asked her to accompany me the rest of my life". (aahhh)

I remember when...

I had taught for two years right out of college and then spent two years as secretary to the pastor and staff where my Don served as Christian Ed director, Youth Director (Jr. Hi, High School AND College) as well as Minister of Music. This was a large church (large for those days) with a very active membership and a sanctuary that seated about 700. Sundays were busy from early morning until after 10 p.m. Wednesday night was prayer and Bible study for the youth, Thursday was choir rehearsal, Friday and Saturday nights were always filled with youth activities, and various church committees met on Monday and Tuesday evenings. Those were exciting and *busy* days. About four years into the marriage, after trying unsuccessfully to get pregnant, we decided to look into adoption. There were very few babies available and many, many hopeful families waiting eagerly for a child but having to wait for years. Well, here's where God comes in and works a miracle. Seven months after we wrote our first inquiry letter, we got our baby. Can you feel the excitement here? We still can—even after nearly 49 years. We had our baby and we were joyful and grateful to God for this marvelous blessing in our lives. About two years later we hoped for a little sister for Glen. God worked a miracle again. Glen was 2 years, 7 months old when we got Connie. She was born on our wedding anniversary but it was fifteen days before we found that out. We had a boy and a girl and now our family was complete—or so we thought. More on this later.....

I remember when...

We received that call late one Friday afternoon from the adoption agency that they had a little girl for us. But wait—she has a heart murmur and a protruding left hip. Do you still want her? *DO WE STILL WANT HER!?!* Immediately we realized that when a child is born to you there are no guarantees. Things in life are not always perfect. Of course we want her! Along with the joy that our new daughter brought us, God heard the pleading of our hearts for a miracle. Monday morning found us in our Pediatrician's office. After thoroughly examining Connie our doctor told us that he could find no evidence of a heart murmur or a protruding left hip. Again God answered our prayers in a miraculous way.

I remember when...

I thought I had the "flu" and it wouldn't go away. So finally, after several weeks I went to the doctor and lo and behold—God had decided to *really* surprise us! He had already heard our heart's cry for a child and had sent us both a boy and a girl. Our lives were now very busy and very fulfilled at this point and we certainly weren't praying for a larger family, but God had other plans. Glen and Connie would be getting a sister or brother. Connie was not yet 13 months old when Donna was born, and were we ever busy parents. God answered that prayer long after we had given up hope. Again—it's a God thing!

I remember when...

Donna was about 8 months old. We were at San Dimas Park celebrating Grandpa Grant's birthday. Donna had reached through the bars of her playpen, grabbed a handful of oak leaves and decided they would make a good lunch. As she began choking, I quickly turned her upside down and reached into her throat to try to get them all out. We immediately left for home and I called the doctor who said she would probably be O.K. and to just watch her. She started running a fever, and her body began to swell. She had been born with a rather large lymphangioma and it had become infected. We had been told it would probably shrink on its own by the time she was a year old, but it hadn't. The doctor took one look at her and said that she needed to be in Children's Hospital L.A. immediately and called to try to get her admitted. When they told him they had no room, he said that he would have to call County Hospital because "these people could never afford what this is going to cost." Little did we realize what lay ahead. He called County and the line was busy so he hung up and just then Children's called back and said to bring her in—that they would put her in the hall. He was not a Christian man, but as he gave us directions he said, "Go, and may God be with you." I said, "Aren't you going to send her in an ambulance?" He told us there wouldn't be anything they could do that we couldn't do, and that she needed us. He added "I hope you get there in time." She was *desperately* ill. Talk about pouring our hearts out to God that whole trip. Well she ended up being in the hospital for 4 months and during that time had four major surgeries, the first two of which the doctors didn't give us much hope of her pulling through. Of course it was a trying time for us, but through it all God gave her a wonderful attitude and a great personality. The nurses and doctors just fell in love with her and called her their little princess. As time progressed she had another 8 major surgeries and today she is a pediatric nurse who takes a real personal interest in all her patients and their families. How good of God to be there and carry us through the great challenges that come our way.

I remember when...

Glen had the chickenpox. He was five years old and there are seldom any complications with chickenpox, but he had an extra-large one on his hip. He was unusually cranky and finally refused to even walk. After a very sleepless night we called the doctor and he told us to bring Glen in. Don took him in and when they didn't return for almost two hours, I began getting really concerned and pulled out a large medical book and started looking up everything I could think of that mentioned symptoms like his. Suddenly my eyes fell on the word *osteomyelitis*. I don't remember ever hearing that word, but after reading up about it a huge scare went through me as I realized his seemed to be a classic case. Then came the call from Don that they were at the hospital and he did have osteomyelitis. The prognosis—they would probably need to operate in three days and the odds were great that he would always be crippled. Wow! Another big challenge since on Monday my husband was to begin a week of qualifying examinations at USC for his doctorate. Our daughter, Donna, also had complications from chickenpox and was in Children's Hospital in Los Angeles. So what do we do? How could he possibly do well on tests during those days so filled with anxiety. So we went to our pastor and another very trusted friend for advice and guidance. Their thought was that he should go on with the exams (the alternative was to wait a whole year before they were offered again) and they would stand by and give me support. Again—LOTS of prayer. Don went on with the testing not telling anyone because he felt they might feel sorry for him and pass him even if he didn't deserve it or have the attitude that *nobody* could do a good job under pressure like that and automatically fail him. Well, God answered prayer BIG TIME. Glen was healed and didn't need surgery after all and there was no crippling. Donna, too, recovered from a severe secondary infection related to the lymphangioma. In addition, Don passed all his tests with flying colors. What a great God we have!  .

I remember when...

The kids were all in school now. In fact, our youngest was in second grade and it was now time for me to get back to teaching after taking about 10 years off to be a stay-at-home Mom. Thinking ahead to college we knew we would have some huge expenses in the next few years. So to get back in the groove, I began subbing. For the last quarter of the year I was asked to take a long-term sub job. The teacher had to leave to have emergency surgery and Open House was coming up fast so it was a major job to get the room looking great for that big occasion. I practically worked day and night for several weeks. On the big night, the principal came through our rooms. After he complimented me on a good job of getting the room ready, I asked, "If someone wanted to teach third grade here next year, what would they need to do?" His reply was, "Oh, all 4 of my third grade teachers are leaving and you can even have your choice of rooms." How's that for an interview? Another wonderful miracle.

I remember when...

The dreaded words came from the doctor—"Yes, it is malignant". Shortly after having had an all-clear from a recent re-take on a mammogram and being told everything was just fine, a "lump" was discovered quite by accident. A yearly physical showed a lump which I couldn't feel, but my doctor said, "You're going for an ultrasound anyway." So prior to the ultrasound I found something in a different spot from what the doctor had found. It was just a funny feeling—a little tight—nothing

I would have ever gone to the doctor for, but since I had to have an ultrasound on the spot the doctor thought she found, I asked about this also. The first one was a cyst but after a doctor's exam, another mammogram, MRI and needle biopsy (all on the same day—another huge miracle), the diagnosis was confirmed. We were to leave on a trip (part business and part pleasure) in two days and were willing to cancel, but the doctor said to go ahead with plans and see the surgeon the day we returned. We were traveling to the east coast to touch base with a musical group from Azusa Pacific University, where my husband had been Academic Vice President and now was Dean of the School of Music (by the time he retired he had served there for 42 years). One of the first stops was at a television broadcast in Canada. The guest speaker that day was marvelous. Afterwards, he came over to the group and asked if he could pray for and anoint with oil our GUIDE who had broken her leg playing soccer and was facing surgery. As the group moved on, Don asked him if he would pray for me, also. As he did, the peace of God came over me and I was really able to go through the whole experience without fear. It turned out my surgeon was a strong Christian. In fact, the morning of surgery he came in to check on me and ask how I was doing. I told him that a lot of people were praying for me and I was anxious to get this over with and go on with life. He said, "Let's pray now," and he held my hand and prayed for me. *God knew the peace that would come over me with that prayer.* Since it was a very small lump and we found it so early, they felt sure there would be no lymph node involvement, but there was, so it was a real miracle the way God led us to find that without waiting a year for the next mammogram (and maybe they wouldn't even have found it then).

I remember when...

A few years later we were surprised to learn that Don had bladder cancer which involved many weeks of treatments using a BCG (live tuberculosis bacteria) to stimulate the immune system so his body will kill the cancer cells. It is often successful, but with no guarantees. As we trusted God with this new challenge, He came through for us again. Frequent check-ups for several years now show him to still be cancer free. Yet another miracle!

So, how about now...

We feel wonderfully blessed with a great family. Not perfect, but much loved. Glen, and Connie with their spouses live in the same town we live in with six of our eight grandchildren. Donna and her husband live in Minnesota with their twins (obviously our "Minnesota Twins"). They all bring much joy along with challenges and add greatly to the quality of our lives. There is not a dull moment! Football, soccer, cross-country, church worship team, musical events (show choir), and the list goes on, give many opportunities to see grandchildren in action.

Yes – I do remember when...

That phrase has been the setting of each point **BUT** from here on out I want to emphasize the present and the future. The focus is now on what I have learned, and what I know. The big lesson is that **God Is Faithful.** His presence is with me every day, no matter what the circumstances. He loves me and I love Him. He will never let me out of His hand. With this fact I face the future with confidence. One of my favorite hymns, GREAT IS THY FAITHFULNESS, tells it all. That hymn reminds me of our certainty for the Future - that with

God's faithfulness He gives "*Strength for today and Bright hope for tomorrow*" as one of the verses says.

**"Strength for today and bright hope
for tomorrow",**

# MY STORY....DELLA ALBRIGHT
## FAITHFUL PRAYERS

It is a long time looking back over my life and as I sit here now facing (as the doctors have told me) less than one year to live, it seems a good time for reflection and putting the story of my life down on paper.

My parents came over from Holland and settled in South Dakota where I was born.  I had two older brothers and one younger sister.  My parents didn't care for the cold and decided that a move out west would be good for the family, so we were on our way.  We settled in Redlands, Ca. where my dad started a Holland bakery and much of our life revolved around the bakery and going to church.  I worked in the bakery from about age 12 to age 17, then ventured out to work for Woolworths. I graduated from high school in 1939, and soon got a job in the Rationing building until the end of World War II.  All during this time my parents took us to a church called the Gospel Hall.  Every Sunday we drove from Redlands to Riverside early in the morning and didn't get back home until 6:30 pm.  The services lasted all day, but sometimes we would leave for the afternoon service and go to the Mission Inn or spend time away just for the afternoon service to break up the day.

When I was 12, my mother died while still in her 40's from an accidental overdose of medication at the hospital where she was staying for a hypoglycemia related illness (misdiagnosed as depression or women's troubles). Around age sixteen I stopped going to church.  I believe that when we were young we were taught that Jesus died on the cross for our sins, I did believe but did not commit my life to serving Jesus .......I, as the prodigal son, went my own way.  I got a job working for an attorney in

Redlands and after two years, married him. It seemed I had everything I would want, a home in Redlands, and another in Newport Beach. Unfortunately, even though we had plenty, our marriage didn't last and after the divorce I moved to Oahu, Hawaii. I worked as assistant manager of a restaurant called The Tropics, and then was manager of the dining room of the officers club on Diamond Head. It was there that I met my second husband, who at that time was a Lt. Commander in the Navy. I then retired from the officers club and enjoyed staying home and planning to build our new home on Diamond Head. We lived there about 8 years, then made the move back to the main land and decided that retiring in Grass Valley was just right for us.

My husband went into real estate and we were able to travel to Europe, Florida, Hawaii, Puerto Rico, and many other places, but as other stories go ours came to an end when my husband found out that he had an inoperable brain tumor. During the time when my husband was sick, we would turn on Dr. Charles Stanley on the TV, and I felt deep inside a draw to come back to the Lord and the teaching that I had as a young girl. As for my husband, I hope that his soul was saved during this time but there was never an outward profession of faith so I can just trust that he heard the salvation story and wait for eternity to know for sure. As for myself, I now see how important it is to be sure of your standing before the Lord and to know that your name is for sure written in the Lamb's Book of Life. ( Rev. 21:27)

Due to the fact that I have cancer of the lungs, I've not been able to go to my church for the past year. Though I'm not able to get around as I did before, I thank the Lord for His blessings and for bringing me back to Him. I am looking forward to seeing Him face to face and being reunited with my family that never stopped praying for me!

# MY STORY..... DONNA ADAMS
# LONGING FOR LOVE

Early in my life as a nine year old, I accepted Jesus Christ as my Savior and had a child-like devotion to Him. Later that year my mother died and someone said that God took her. Bitterness began at that time toward God. For some reason financial or other, my Dad left four of us children with relatives and I believe that created an emotional block that kept me from growing up emotionally. Therefore it caused me to long for love above all things.

Let me share a little of my experience in finding love........

I spent the first thirty years of my life in longing and in loneliness though it was not necessary, for I could have turned to God's word sooner. Jer. 31:3, I kept God waiting......

The Lord taught me how He heals broken hearts and with spiritual growth came emotional growth. Some years later I was able to share with others who also had broken hearts that His Word is how He heals.

Jer. 15:16-19, I learned His love would come to me through His Word and not through others. I learned there are two spirits in me, mine and God's. I learned there are two loves in me, mine and His. I learned there are two lives in me, mine and His. I learned to separate them in my mind for as He said "one is precious and one is vile."

Then He taught me to love as He does, by having the grace to forgive all others for His sake and so I could be free of guilt and bitterness and learn to live in the grace of His love. Heb. 12:15, Lk. 7:46

In order to live in the light of His love instead of the dark, our hearts and minds must always focus first on the One who is all we need, for God Himself is love and we cannot love others "at all times" until we experience this love our self. Eph. 3:17-19, IJn. 4:7-12 and Heb.13:5-9.

In God's creation of mankind He created them in His image, filled with divine perfect eternal love and with perfect knowledge. Because they yielded to the temptation to want more, they lost the inner image of the Spirit of a God of love and became an empty self like Satan. Then they gave birth in their fallen image to an empty self-centered proud and angry child, revealing the loss of God's spiritual love in the human heart.

When we accept the Lord Jesus Christ as our Savior we are then re-created as new creatures in His Spiritual image again, but we still retain our self-centered loves until we can grow enough in His truth and His grace to deny our old self-centered control and let our new life take control. I learned that growing in grace and truth will cause this new kind of love to grow and enlarge in our hearts. Our longing and hungering for love will continue and help us seek the Lord until we realize the love of God comes to us as we learn to live in the Word and we get our joy from His beautiful promises of care and eternal love and forgiveness.

The more we experience of the love for God and for others, the more joy and love fills us and relieves the longing and need we once felt. The more we forgive, as we were forgiven the less anger and bitterness we feel as His love and grace takes their place in our hearts. Eph. 4:30-32, I Jn. 1:3-4

By accepting His love through forgiveness, we feel His approval and love so we express our love the same way, by forgiving others as He forgave us. This is obedience to His will, just as Christ's love led Him to obey His Father's will, which was to die for and restore the lost and lonely and rescue those empty souls who would otherwise "long for love" forever, but would be separated from His love forever. IJn 2:5, Rom. 4:7-8.

God is the only source of true and "eternal love" in the world, which He has made available to us all through the sacrifice of His Son. The Lord showed me that with every circumstance that came into my life, God trusts me to handle it with "not my will, but Thine be done!" This is the denial of self that puts Christ in control and is our greatest love for Him.

Under God's hand my life became a ministry of teaching spiritual maturity in Campus Crusade for Christ, many ladies Bible studies and later on as a pastor's wife. God lead me to teach in Garden Grove, CA, Santa Ana, CA. and later on in Phoenix and now in Payson, Arizona. I praise and thank God for his faithfulness in my life!

# MY STORY.....LYNNE CASTLE

As far back as I can remember, I had one dream, to be a mother. I loved babies and in my youth, I did not think much past the part of having and loving a baby.

I married when I was 21. In 1974, that seemed old. I was running out of time. I had endometriosis which I had had since I was 15. I did not know if I would be able to conceive and as it turned out, my condition made it difficult. I had already had various procedures and drug treatments before I was married to alleviate the pain I experienced. I had been told that my odds of getting pregnant were slim. After I was married I had two major surgeries. During the second surgery, my left tube and ovary were removed. In 1976, I became pregnant. If you have ever experienced infertility, you will understand the elation my husband and I felt. My female problems had been going on for a long time. We had not been given much hope. We were and still are Christians. We prayed for a miracle and the Lord gave us one.

Sarah Lynne was born May 6, 1977. She was 7 weeks pre-mature. She appeared to be perfect, just small. At U.C.L.A., in 1977, it was protocol to do immune testing on the premature babies. Her cells did not respond properly and for weeks they thought it was laboratory error. At the age of eight weeks she was diagnosed with Severe Combined Immune Deficiency. It is an immuno-suppressive disease that prohibited her from fighting off infection. We were told that she would not live many more days. This was baffling to us. Why would the Lord give us this child to be taken away? Questions. Sarah defied the odds and lived longer than expected. The first year she spent most of her time in the hospital in reverse isolation. We had to wear mask and gowns to be with her. I was with her every day. My husband would come after work and so would my parents. I had an aunt that spent many days with me at the hospital and it meant so much to me. The second year we took three trips to Wisconsin for her to have thymus epithelium transplants. The hope was that the healthy pieces of thymus put into her leg would replace what she was missing in her immune system and enable her white cells to function. Sarah died on September 26, 1979. It was a shock. She had beaten so many infections. When I was told that she was going to die, I did not believe it. I should say, I did not want to believe it. When you conceive a child, you immediately start to dream of what they will be like. Will they go to college? Will they get married? Will you cry when they go to kindergarten? When you are told they are going to die, you get stuck. Your world turns upside down. What was once normal is now so removed. You function day to day. You are afraid to continue your hopes and dreams. You forget them. Your life stops. You are engulfed in this medical puzzle and trying to comprehend what is happening. You tell yourself what the doctors are saying is going to happen just can't be. I always thought the doctors were going to tell me they had been wrong and made a mistake, but that did not happen. I was not prepared for her death. I just could not believe she actually died. I have to say that during Sarah's illness, we had wonderful, caring doctors. They spent hours with us. They said she was a pioneer in this field. They were learning from her. We read and read in order to understand what was happening in her little body. She was such a fighter with a sweet sweet spirit.

I had a very difficult time after Sarah's death. My lifelong dream of being a mother was over. We were told not to have more children as they may have this same disorder. We had a home with four bedrooms. We had planned on a large family. This did not make sense. Our thoughts are not God's thoughts; we do not know His plan. (For my thoughts are not your thoughts. ...Isaiah 55:8). I did not want to go on. I was deeply depressed. My husband told me I was being selfish as he was hurting too and he needed me. He was absolutely right. Grief is a very selfish emotion. We are only thinking of our pain. We are not thinking of others. It is difficult to convince yourself that your two and one-half year old is better off in heaven than with you. I am sure that it is true, but for me, it was difficult. It was not comforting at the time.

We decided we would attempt adoption. That was the safe thing to do. We learned quickly that that is easier said than done. We made phone calls to many agencies. We told them our story and they were sympathetic but not encouraging. We told everyone we knew.

We began going to a Bible Study with some people that worked with my husband. It was held in the home of a woman that was a labor and delivery nurse in a hospital. The first night I met her, I told her of our desire. She already knew about us and told me not to be hopeful. They had very few babies that were given up for adoption and when they were, the county took them. Once the county had them in their system it was a two-year wait. This particular night we had a prayer session that was unforgettable. The spirit of the Lord was there. Even the men were weeping. These precious people were weeping for our loss and asking the Lord to work a miracle. I felt such a peace. I felt so much love.

Two weeks from this night, I had a phone call at work. This woman had called my husband at work crying. She told him that she was doing the intake on an expectant mom with a doctor and the doctor told her that this mom did not want this baby. He asked her if she knew anyone that would want a baby. This had never happened to her before. She said she felt God was using her. She was crying when she called Wayne at work. She had never experienced anything like this before. Four weeks later, Lisa was born on July 24, 1980. If you think about it, Sarah died 9/26/79 and Lisa was born 7/24/80. The Lord was already sending Lisa to us when Sarah went to be with Him. Again, His plans are not known to us (Isaiah 55:8).

We were involved in a Bible Study through church and getting involved in working with the youth once again. We had been youth leaders early in our marriage before Sarah was born. I had claimed Psalms 37: 4, "Delight yourself in the Lord and He will give you the desires of your heart." I felt that although Sarah was gone, we now had Lisa. I was so blessed with this perfect and healthy little girl. I felt the Lord had given me the desire of my heart, to be a mom.

I wish I could say we lived happily ever after but life is a continuing challenge. In November of 1981, I was diagnosed with malignant melanoma. It was a very scary time for me. I was told that I could die. I had wanted to die when Sarah died but now I had this baby girl and all was right with the world, not now. Once again, I was confused. My thoughts immediately go to God. Why did He give us Lisa and now I might die. My melanoma was on my arm and I had to have surgery at John Wayne Cancer Clinic. My lymph nodes were clear but they gave me many warnings. One of these warnings was to not have any babies for at least 2 years (they now tell people to not ever become pregnant). I thought this was a long shot inasmuch as I am the infertile queen. For the first time in our marriage, we were using birth control. We had never done that before. We did not use birth control after Sarah died. We did not think we would get pregnant that easily. We took our chances and then adopted. We now began using birth control as the doctors said if there was one cell of melanoma left in my body and I became pregnant, I could die. Melanoma is sensitive to estrogen.

I became very sick in July and August of 1982. I was seen every three months by the oncologist. They checked everything. I had chest x-rays on a regular basis, urinalysis and blood work. Always looking for the cancer to return. The doctor asked me if I could be pregnant. I was shocked. I said there was no way this could happen. They wanted to do a blood test. They said if I were pregnant I would have to have an abortion. I knew this was not possible. At the same time, I was upset to say the least. Please don't tell me you (God) are going to give me a baby that the doctors tell me I should not carry. I struggled with this for a few days but knew it just could not happen. My oncologist called me one afternoon and asked how I was feeling. I told him not well. He then told me I was pregnant and he wanted me to come in right away to have an abortion. All at once, I was flooded with the presence of the Holy Spirit. I had a peace that passes all understanding ("And the peace of God which surpasses all comprehension ..." Philippians 4:7). I told the doctor I could not abort because I do not believe in abortion. I also knew in my heart that this baby was a gift from God. The doctor gave me all the medical reasons why I needed to have an abortion. I then asked him if he knew about Sarah. He did not. I told him about her. I asked him what he would tell me if I were his wife and he said I was not being fair. I told him that I knew this baby was from God. This was a gift. Needless to say, I did not have an abortion.

Now I had to tell Sarah's doctors. One of them also wanted me to abort as he felt it was a 1 in 3 chance of the disorder reoccurring. He was a very compassionate man and did not want us to go through the loss again. He meant well. I told him this baby was a gift from God and the destiny of the child was in God's hands. He accepted that. The other doctor was happy for us and wanted to be there for the birth. Christopher Wayne was born March 9, 1983. A son, and he was perfect. I had wanted a son (Psalms 37:4). Sarah's pediatrician watched the procedure, as it was a cesarean section, thru a small window of the surgery room. He then took Christopher away from us to examine him and make sure he had a good immune system. He was given a clean bill of health.

One thing I have learned throughout my life is that worrying does us no good. The Lord tells us not to worry. If He can take care of the birds of the air, He will take care of us. We can change nothing by worrying. I spent over a year of my life worrying that my melanoma would return and I would die (Luke 12:25). It did not happen. I journaled when I was pregnant with Chris. There were days when I doubted my decision. I knew I could never have had an abortion but I worried about the baby's health. What if he did have the immune problem? I had moments of doubt.

Lisa came into my life when I was drowning in sorrow. My arms felt so empty. She was my lifesaver. God sent her to us. I had so much love in my heart to give to her. She was perfect. We have always told her that. She was our rainbow at the end of the storm after Sarah died. When she became a teenager, things got very difficult. She did some serious rebelling. Those were very hard times. That is another story.

Christopher was a gift. Just given to us because God wanted to fulfill another desire of my heart, having a son. I never imagined that we would have more children. God tells us in Isaiah 55:8. His thoughts are not our thoughts. God is so good. He loves us so much. Our faith was strengthened. We had to trust the Lord with all our heart, soul and mind to believe this baby was going to be well and I would be well. Chris was our rainbow after the storm of my cancer.

Life has so many ups and downs. We never know what will happen around the next corner. We can never take a day for granted. We need to praise God for each day. We need to praise God for our health, for the health of our children, our family.

In 2003 my sister was diagnosed with colon cancer, stage 4. I knew she was very sick long before she would go to a doctor but she would not listen. She was a very strong-minded person. By the time we got her to a doctor, the cancer was everywhere. She lived 8 months. My parents, myself and my husband helped with her care. She was 49 when she died. She claimed a healing as soon as she was diagnosed until about a month before she died. She had scriptures all over her home. We could not talk about her illness. She believed this was a diagnosis by man. God is the great physician and He had the power to heal her. I know that to be true. I believe He healed her on September 15, 2003 when she stopped breathing and went to be with the Lord. This was a very painful time. She was my younger sister. I did everything I could to make her last days comfortable. For those of us that have been caregivers, it is heart wrenching.

On April 12, 2006, my first grandchild was born. Lisa had a daughter, Presley Jo (another rainbow) She named her after her Aunt Robin Jo, my sister. It was not until I experienced a grandmother's love that I realized the pain my mother must have felt when Sarah died. Sarah was my daughter and her granddaughter. At the time of Sarah's death, I thought only of my pain. How selfish I was. My poor mom lost her daughter at the age of 49 and her heart was so broken. We all were broken. It took this experience to realize the pain my own mother suffered at the loss of her first grandchild. All these trials are learning experiences. With pain comes growth or should I call it maturity?

Life goes on and we live each day to the fullest. We have challenges within our families. We have challenges at our job. It is difficult to live in this world in the best of circumstances. When we hit the bumps, we have to call upon our Father in Heaven to pull us through. Sometimes we run the other way and stomp our feet. It does no good. He waits until we are ready to receive His love and He wraps His arms around us and comforts us. I believe He cries with us. This life is short compared to eternity and I believe it is a testing ground. I have not always done so well. I love the Lord. I try and show that to others. There are so many hurting people. I know in my own life, the pain is more tolerable with the Father's arms around me. The healing comes only with His help. The hope of seeing our loved ones that have gone before us is only in His promise of eternal life. I know I will see my Sarah and my sister again. We will all be together for eternity.

# MY STORY.......MYRNA TUCKLEY

Am I There Yet? Have I Done Enough?

It seems that during my life I have been on a continual journey to a destination that was consciously unknown to me. But my inner self, or perhaps it could be better described as my subconscious thoughts and feelings, felt strongly this wasn't it; I wasn't there yet. There? Where was there? There was a place that I would be accepted, wanted, loved, approved of and maybe respected or admired just a little. For my entire life I have never felt valued, enough. Way deep inside of me is a yearning to finally be "there". I know now that "there" is the peace I have been given that is found in the knowledge that God loves me, accepts me as I am and was valuable enough for Him to give up His life for me, His child. And, that He loved me enough to willingly suffer on the cross that I might be "there" in Heaven with Him for Eternity.

You see, I know in my heart and to the very core of my soul that being "there" with God is a reality and I know that the Holy Bible, His Word, promises that I do not have to do anything special to get there, for He accepts me for who I am, wants me to be with Him. One day, when I see His glorious face He will assure me that He has understood my needs and has been pleased by my continually striving to be all that He wants me to be. When I finally get there with Him, my deepest desire is that He says to me, "well done, my child". Because then it will be enough. The combined learning experiences He has allowed during my life while He was always there holding my hand so wouldn't fall all the way down, have challenged me all along the way to keep climbing, to get "there" because there is a better place than we have ever known here on earth. I believe that with my entire mind, my heart, and my soul.

Due to my very painful childhood experiences and the knowledge that I have since gained in His Word, I know in my heart I am God's child but it is very difficult for me to relate to me Lord and Savior that I love as my Father. I have never known a man as a father here on earth, so I really do not know what loving or being loved by a Father feels like. As my story unfolds, you will also discover I have never ever been given many good reasons to trust any man to keep his promises. As an adult, I can worship, obey and love my Lord and Savior because I have life experiences that have imbedded those feelings in my heart. But there was absolutely nothing in my childhood to help me feel protected, loved or cherished by a father.

The memories I have of my childhood are disturbing and confusing when I think of them. As with all of us, the beginning years of infancy through puberty established lifelong reactions to experiences and formed the patterns that designed the remainder of my years.

Today, the child inside me determines my responses to some distinct emotional triggers. For example, the instability of having a teen mother who had been abandoned by a husband ten years her senior and who resented being left wholly responsible for me proved many years later to, following many, many miserable early childhood experiences result in a child growing into an adult that continued to feel undeserving, abandoned, guilty and insecure. Some of what I explain later in this chapter will enlighten you as to the truth behind this strong statement.

My Mother had been raised by a strict disciplinarian who would not let her return home with a baby after she had run away and eloped. He felt she had made her bed, so to speak, so, she needed to find menial work at the young age of seventeen; ending up with the miserable job of ironing sheets in a laundry and having to leave me foster care for the first seven years of my life. On what I can remember as only occasionally, she would pick me up to be with her for the weekends. During these times I remember being told how much she loved me, but those terms of endearment are overshadowed by memories of unfair expectations of perfect behavior and severe physical punishment if the behavior wasn't what she wanted it to be. I also remember that she loved to dress me up on those occasions and have me sing or recite by memory for her friends. It seemed to me then, if my performances disappointed her, she would scold me harshly and then promptly return me to foster care. I felt she was ashamed of me. I soon learned that in order to be wanted, accepted, loved and not be abused, you needed to not complain and always do everything as perfect as you can. I learned you had to earn all those good feelings. I became a very disciplined and good little girl.

Mother was pursuing in earnest, during those years the fun and freedom of being emancipated by entertaining the military during World War II at the USO Clubs. My loving grandmother would see to it, though, that when I could I was taken to church.

It is important to mention at this point, that my Mother had been active in church as a child. Her mother was a devout born-again Christian who struggled to raise four girls while my grandfather drove a cross-country moving van and was not at home on any consistent basis. My Mother was the church pianist and in a Christian trio that sang on the radio before she ran away to get married. I have heard she continued these activities during my early years, but I have no memory of it at all. It must have been my Grandmother who first told me about Jesus, when I would have opportunity to stay with her. I do know when I think of going to church, I only remember being there with my grandmother. I imagine some of my early days were filled with stories of Jesus and memorizing Bible verses and songs I will forever thank my grandmother for giving me the gift of the knowledge of Jesus Christ who was caring for me and protecting me all those confusing years. I must have bonded with God at that time.

These years were the beginning strokes of what was to be the design pattern of my life; feelings of instability, insecurity, fear, confusion and never feeling I could ever be good enough to get "there". "There" at that time was someplace where the other kids at my foster homes and in Sunday school seemed to be, happy and safe where people always loved them.

I was so excited, at the age of eight, when my Mother took me to California to live, All the day's we drove, traveling in my grandfather's cross-country moving van from state to state, she would tell me stories of how there was a daddy waiting there for me and how she would be able to take care of me; I would not be alone again. I believed her enthusiastic promises that when we got "there" I would be with her always in our very own house and I would have the father I had never had. I thought it sounded wonderful to be there and fathers must be very special people if you had to drive seven days to find one. But as it turned out, I was desperately disappointed again. My Mother soon discovered that after having me in the house, her new husband had decided he didn't want children around his house, after all. Unfortunately, in her eagerness to marry and be taken care of herself, she had lived in hopes that I would be accepted by him. I had promised my mother I would be a very good girl so she wouldn't ever have to leave me again, but I couldn't be good enough. He wouldn't answer me if I called him Daddy, allowed his dog to frighten and attack me, ignored me most of the time if he wasn't cruelly teasing me and would ridicule me in ways that were humiliating and very hurtful whenever my mother was not around.

I am sure all my childhood experiences were not bad; my mother was not a wicked woman. Years later, following Christian counseling, I learned she also needed to be loved by a man very badly, having been abandoned by two significant men in her life, and would often do whatever she felt she needed in order to feel wanted and loved. So, she continued to urge me to behave perfectly, never ever do anything to upset my step father because our getting to stay "there" was conditional on my behavior in time, my stepfather required that my mother go to work again to pay for all of my expenses, so I was given excessive household responsibilities that had to be done all of the time I was not in school. I was not allowed playtimes or any friends at the house. By the third grade, I cooked, cleaned, laundered and related very much to the story of Cinderella. I was so insecure "there" that I tried very hard not to make any mistakes in order to prove I was valuable enough to be accepted by my stepfather and her.

After many separations in their marriage, it became very clear to me. I just wasn't capable of being perfect enough to be wanted or valued. I became very timid and shy, accustomed to being alone at home. Going to school was also very difficult. The other children would laugh at my answer when the teacher would call on me and I didn't understand why. I didn't know then that I had lost all but 30 percent of my hearing when I was being disciplined at the age of two.

My mother had a complete nervous breakdown when I was ten. From then on, she relied on me to cope on my own, and we switched roles. I became the Mother and she became the daughter. During that year, she left me with my stepfather's mother and when we would go to visit her, I was only allowed to peek at her in her straight jacket through a tiny window at the hospital. I was so frightened because I thought maybe I was responsible for her being in there. I was afraid of what would happen to me if she never came out of that room.

I have not detailed many of the painful experiences I suffered as a child, only enough to try and explain a life-long see saw of ups and downs and how God was always my Guiding Light, though I was not fully aware of it. For example, at the age of 12, my stepfather put me on a train and had me make the three-day trip to Indiana to where my mother was staying. I remember I had to find my bags at the Chicago station and transfer to another station and then find the train all by myself. I remember that experience as the most frightening and alone time in my life. I knew then, my mother was right; I must learn to cope on my own. Years later, my job required I travel alone all over the United States to speak as a conference presenter for many years. God must have been preparing me for this part of my adult life even then. What an awesome God He is, He knows every hair on our head and every step our life will take; even before we are born.

Through adolescence and into my teen years my life was just as full of confusing episodes in my home life and the unstable insecure times of never knowing where home was again, just as in my younger years. During those six years my mother and step-father separated more than ten times and re-married twice. In between, there were many, many other men my mother used to fill the void of love in her life. I was very active in a youth group at church and this is when I asked Jesus to be my Lord and Savior. I know now, I didn't fully understand what that meant or what was in store for my life from then on. I had a long way to travel and many lessons to learn before I was "there".

My mother and I had truly switched roles by the time I entered high school. She was the victim that needed me for survival. I needed her to need me so I felt valuable. It was a relationship I felt comfortable with. I had become the mother; the one who would wait up at night to be sure she was in from a date and safe for the night, care for her during her physical illnesses, her psychological and emotional seizures and make endless visits to the hospital when she was sick or confined. I would continue to make the highest grades while maintaining the household so she would find me necessary in her life. I thought that maybe if I was outstanding, I could even make her be proud of me as a student and a daughter. Sometimes I would study all night, because I was afraid if I didn't make a good grade on a test I would be punished or I would make her sick and she would go away again. She was my only security and by this time I had become totally co-dependent. By then my mother had fully established a mindset and spent a lifetime of being unable to cope and was often too sick to work or she would break down again. I felt so guilty that I couldn't ever be quite good enough to please her no matter how hard I tried and that was why she kept getting sick; so I just kept trying to get "there" to the place of approval and acceptance. Life just kept moving forward in that fashion. Isn't it strange how life destroying habits fall into place so naturally?

In my junior year of high school, I met a boy who needed me as much as my mother did. He had gotten into all kinds of trouble in his hometown, so was sent by his parents to live with his aunt in the town where I lived. When he arrived at school one day, I thought he was the most handsome boy I had ever seen, and I heard all the girls at school wanted a date with him.

I decided then and there that if I could win him over them that I would really be admired and feel special. Besides, this was certainly the Prince I had imagined all these years would rescue me, just like Cinderella. While getting to know him, I discovered he had all the needy habits I had become used to in people I was close to. I was very comfortable with him because of that. I met his needs too; it was almost too perfect. I believed all his excuses. I would be the one he would come to when he needed me to write notes to get him back in school when he was truant, do his homework when he didn't and cover for him when he was out drinking at night, had lied or stayed out all night. I know now that I was ready and waiting emotionally to pretend this was a perfect relationship for me. I became very valuable to him and he depended on me. As I look back on it, I believe my becoming his girlfriend was just one more codependent relationship, but at the time I thought I had won the prize others hadn't, so I felt special. I knew how to win him over to me; I'd work hard for him and forgive him just as I had for my mother. It had worked with the only other relationship I had in my life. The other girls could go to college, I couldn't. Even though my grades qualified me for a number of scholarships to college, I now had two people who needed me and besides my mother could not afford college expenses. We were engaged at fifteen.

I pretended to everyone to be happy because I felt so lucky someone finally wanted me. My boyfriend lived with me and my mother during my senior year as he had graduated the year before and he didn't want to go home. He liked the treatment he got at my house better. I tried to break up with him once, after we were engaged due to his misbehavior and his not working during that year, but he sat in my driveway for four days until I would take the ring back! I guess I felt he must really want and love me to do such a thing. I gave in and we continued the same old pattern of his not coping and my forgiving and saving him.

My boyfriend said if we did not get married after high school, his parents would send him to the Navy. I remember feeling much the same with him as I did with my mother; needed. Once we were married, I was determined I would never divorce, because my children were going to always have a home to call their own and they would always have both a mother and father. I now had a chance to escape my unhappy past and I looked forward to providing for my children all the love and security I had never had. At the same time, my husband said he looked forward to being his own boss and never being told no again, like he was told by his parents. Talk about being unequally yoked!

My husband asked my mother to join us on our honeymoon, and the three of us continued to live together. While we were all sharing a house, my husband broke his arm doing ice-skating with mother, and lost his new job. Since my mother was out work, I supported and cared for the three of us for a while. I became pregnant two months after I was married. With my taking on new responsibilities and not going to be living with her, my mother and stepfather married again and a few months after my son born.

From the beginning of my marriage, my life was much the same as it had been all my life, so far, with mother. My husband continued to drink, gamble and try all sorts of new expensive hobbies like auto drag racing. He loved me very much, he said, but he just wasn't as happy being stable like I was, so he needed me to be the steady foundation of our marriage. He was very charming and could be very persuasive, just as my mother could. He made me feel necessary to his well-being, so I felt good about taking care of him and our child. Again, I was so confused. My life seemed to be exactly as it had always been. I felt so wholly responsible and my child was my only joy. I was unhappy in my marriage.

When my son was four, I found I was pregnant with our second child. I decided right then that no matter what I was feeling; I would stay in this marriage forever and provide my children with the stability and security I never had. I determined my children would never have to be faced with a stepfather! My children would not have the unhappy life I had experienced so far.

When my daughter was nine months old, I finally succumbed to the need to find a job away from home to meet our mounting expenses. From the beginning, I found work part-time in the evenings and on Saturday that would allow my husband to be at home so our children would not need a baby-sitter; one of us would be with them.

This decision to work during his off hours resulted in my husband and I not having much time together, which seemed to work better and better for our entire marriage. Work became a form of escape from our constant marriage problems and our extreme differences for both of us. My mother was still leaving one man for another, and from time to time, they would deliver her back to my doorstep. She had now developed a strong addiction to prescription drugs. S he would desperately call me for help repeatedly out of need, when she was under the influence of drugs and alcohol or had been tossed aside by the man she was with at the time. It was then she quit going to church.

We were Sunday Christians then, as I had always been, but not knowing what that meant at the time. It was then we learned about Bible prophesy. These revelations scared my husband so much he wanted to stay home from church and watch all the Bible Prophecy programs on Sunday he could find. He talked a lot about the end coming, but it didn't change his lifestyle. I listened, and I read. I knew God was becoming a very necessary part of my life, but I still put Him on the shelf when I needed to, in order to keep up with our faster and faster pace of living. I was desperately seeking answers. We started going to a drive-in church on Sunday mornings, because that way we could go to church in our pajamas and the he could get to work on part -time jobs in the garage and we could separately do what needed to be to keep up our home. God was a part of lives when we remembered to pray, or when I prayed for help out of hurt. Neither one of us understood we owed a debt to God or that we needed to do anything special to thank him for what He was giving us.

We were both so busy with our own concept of what marriage and family was, our everyday life just kept happening and the years went by. I lived my life to do my best work help keep my family together, no matter what it took. That was my biggest mistake, "no matter what it took". The secular world became much more important that God's plan for my life. I thought I had it all under control. I became the Director of a private fashion college and modeling school and agency. I ran all three businesses for an absentee owner who was always very sick and needed me to manage things for her. Does this sound familiar? My profession was such that I dressed in suits, hats and gloves every day. This took time. The demands of my responsibilities required time and organization. I would plan one day for me to spend with the children, one as a family day for us all to be together, and work the rest of the days. I loved my children more than anything and I was so proud of them. Now I know that at the time they were more aware of the time spent away from them. Also, I had fallen into my mother's habit in that I had given them more responsibilities at home than their friends had. They resented that but they never have complained. I resented the time I had to be away from them. I blamed my husband for that. He settled into working very hard for money to support his weekend bad habits and his family. He even had two jobs during the years he was drag racing. Then he added part-time jobs so we could have more things and more fun.

Our houses grew bigger, luxury cars and race cars became more important, our kid's sports and activities with their friends increased my hours working increased, and the poker games and celebration parties with his friends away from home increased for my husband. We were busy, wealthy, and looked to others like the perfect family.

Over the years, I had become very successful at the work I was doing. I was earning a great deal of money so therefore very easily led into a full-time career. I was very well-known in my profession and enjoyed a reputation as a successful businesswoman. I had become used to doing everything perfectly and working very hard, no matter what cost to me. So, my week days and evenings were filled with my career, and my off-hours were being at home.

For more than twenty-five years our marriage was a continual roller-coaster.

Except that our children had grown into fine, beautiful young people, nothing else changed in our lives. The pattern of our co-dependent life together had been determined. I would be the mother and provider, he would be the little bad boy that was always sorry that I would continue to forgive and cover for. I covered his gambling debts, his excuses when he had relationships with other women, excuses for him when he was drinking. I protected our children, friends and other parents and community from the truth, exactly as I had done all my life for my mother and me. I was so used to pretending that there were times I even believed it. Everyone we knew thought our marriage was perfect. My husband said he thought so too. After all, he loved me and needed me. So, balancing an unpredictable marriage, children, church attendance, a professional career and a very needy mother gave me a sense all was right with my world and I took a lot of pride in doing it all well. We owned a three-acre estate; owned a business and the building and were considered very wealthy and had respect in the community. We had it all, and we were "there". I thought I knew what life was all about. My mother was still very much an obstacle in my daily life, but she had married my father-in-law following my husbands' mother's death, so even she was being taken care of at the time.

But we weren't "there"; we were "there" only by the world's standards. So, why was I not happy? Isn't that just when God allows us to fall, when we think we are doing it all ourselves? Didn't we deserve all we had sacrifices and worked so hard for? We forgot that without the gifts God bestows on us we have nothing.

Slowly and over time, I began to be overwhelmed with the thought God wanted more of me. I had some lessons I needed to learn. I couldn't sleep. I felt so pressured. I knew God wanted something of me, there was something I needed to do, but I didn't know what it was. I read every Christian book I could. I felt uneasy about charging families thousands of dollars for training that would lead their sons and daughters into a profession that had changed so radically since I had begun working in the field. I questioned the new moralities in the world of professional modeling. The owner of the business was not entirely honest regarding her income and had appointed me her financial manager as well.

I felt strongly that I had to choose between God's way and the way we were headed; the world's way. I left my career to work in the office of my husband's business in the hopes that I could increase the income of his cabinet and door business and give more support to our marriage and family. I told my husband I thought God wanted the wife and mother to be in the home and to be a good helpmate. I wanted to really get to know my children as young adults, while they were still at home. I was making a huge amount of money at this time. But, I thought what could he say? I did it for him and our family? Little did I know what he had been up to all those years when we were so busy building our lives as they were?

My husband panicked when I made those statements and no longer shouldered so much responsibility. He liked our life as it was. His lifestyle of wine, women and fast living which I didn't have full knowledge of, had become too important to him. He allowed me the opportunity of discovery. Our company was failing from his neglect and lack of interest.

He decided to sell his business and the building, sell our home and give up the relationship with his family. His plan was to invest what his half of the community property could bring him to live the easy life with a woman he was seeing at the time. His words were: he needed to sell us because he wanted the money. I was devastated. The shell that formed the facade that held us together was broken and all that was ugly in it began to pour out of our lives for all to see. I only thank God that my children were married and had begun their own lives by that time and were not too directly affected. However, all my confidence was shattered. I had been able to keep my marriage whole by serving others and my family. I had read so many Christian books on God's plan for a good marriage. I had learned to submit to my husbands' wishes and decisions. Why didn't God's way work for me? I was lost, confused and felt totally alone. I knew God was my only hope. I could not control the events in my life by serving people and meeting their needs. I had lost my way; I wasn't going to get "there" ever by myself.

All I knew to do was turn to God and pray. I had redirected my life to follow God's teachings and promised to give my heart and soul to Him. I truly gave up my will and died to the world and soon after lost most of my worldly possessions. I was really confused. I thought my life would be better with God in charge. Instead, I was without all I had held dear to me. My job, career, home and children at home to care for were all gone. I learned God gives and God takes away. For many years, he had not been my first priority...I found I now had plenty of time to focus on finding a way through the deepest hurts I had experienced yet. Once again, I relived all the doubts and fears of who I was, what I was worth, and who could I trust. I read, I sought Christian counsel, I listened and I prayed. At times, my heart felt like someone was reaching down my throat and pulling it out. My heart ached. How very much deeper adult hurts are; they slice into your whole being.

Praise God! He brought me through my despair answering my sincere prayers. He gave me the wisdom to reason, the strength to bear all things, and assurances through His Word, messages and songs.

For one year, I stayed in a part of our home while my husband lived in another. I was determined to demonstrate Christianity and pray for my husband to change his mind and reunite our family. He didn't. In fact, I would often return home from work to find him and the other woman enjoying our home together. That was very hurtful, especially when I would be asked to join them for a meal in my kitchen. I moved out when it was too much for me to endure.

I began attending church in a beach city where my mother and stepfather (formerly my father-in-law) lived. I spent many week-ends with the two of them and my aunt who lived next door. My mother was happy for the first time in her life.

I opened a small business in my apartment with a friend and former employee. I looked for a job teaching in public schools. That is when I found out I needed to go to college after all. I had been issuing college degrees for many years at the private trade college, but I hadn't taken the time to earn a degree myself. I was able to obtain a teaching position at a local vocational school teaching Fashion Merchandising, but I needed to keep my business going also in order to pay off all the expenses we had incurred through the divorce, close his business and support myself. These were very humbling experiences. I also began teaching in the Marketing department of a local community college.

Our company, a sales and fashion promotion / merchandise display business was slow to start. We produced dress-for-success seminars for corporations, did seasonal merchandise display and advertising tabloids for department stores and shopping centers every week-end. In the evenings, I would go to college. I was working seven days per week from 8 AM to 11 PM. I do not know if I was running away from my emotions or frantically trying to build some kind of new life. I just know I kept myself busier and busier until I ceased to find time to read the Bible again, to pray or to listen to God. I couldn't even seem to find time to go to church regularly. In my heart I felt like I was still a Christian and loved God and wanted to live to please Him. But, I must have thought God understood and I knew He was there when I needed Him. I just didn't need Him quite so much as I had right after the divorce. This is a mistake many of us often make. We only turn to God when we have no one else to turn to. God is so patient with us. He knows what the outcome of our life will be before we are born, but He allows us free will to choose, and our human nature doesn't surprise Him.

My daughter began to work in her church office, and my son played on the church baseball team with his Pastor. I felt comfortable they were fine, spiritually too. I wasn't concerned about their relationship with God. We all believed we were saved and God was protecting and guiding us daily. I thought to myself I had done my job as a parent, nurturing their spirituality while they were young. How smug and self-sufficient we can become when we are not hurting or think we need as much help from God.

Because I was working so many hours at the time, my aunt introduced my partner and me to an architect who had experience and an interest in designing for stage productions. He decided to come to see one of our week-end shows and he was hooked. He loved it all; the shows and being around the models too. He was soon designing, building and helping us set up for the shows and the fashion events and seminar. This man was in the United States with his architectural firm that was home-based in England. He was scheduled to leave to go back to England soon, so questions about how involved he should remain in the company began to surface. We decided he would leave his job and become a partner in the business. He would live at the beach with my parents and together we could build the business to cover his personal living expenses. As I look back on it now, what a perfect set up for me the caregiver! I now had found another person to depend on me and help support. He also said he needed to pay child support and alimony to an ex-wife in Canada. He and I had grown very close and I assumed I was important to him. I reasoned that if I worked even harder he would appreciate me that much more! It made perfectly good sense. I thought this was an opportunity to build a career and a new life with someone who valued me.

I wanted this relationship to be right with God so He would honor the relationship and bless it. I explained to this man how important being equally yoked in God's eyes was to me. And, when I did he said he had gone to church in England but listening to me he now wanted to be born-again and become a Christian. I was so happy. I just knew God had brought me this man of my dreams. He was educated, sophisticated, and so sensitive to my feelings and he shared my love of the fashion industry and the art world. He was everything my first husband wasn't. I had seen what a good parent he was to his own children when he was with them and my children and family really approved of our becoming closer. He and I would talk for hours, planning our future together. I felt wonderful. I borrowed money to rent an office, buy supplies and office furniture. His interest and creative technical skills supported my creative ideas and writings. He even understood my time away from him to go to school.

We eloped to Mexico and were married one week-end when a show was cancelled. While I was still teaching full and part-time our business grew quickly into a national business producing educational teaching aids for fashion/marketing teachers, a color analysis and fashion consulting firm, and a product manufacturing business for professional fashion/image consulting supplies and sales tools. I became a corporate color consultant and the national color spokesperson for a paint manufacturer during school breaks. Of course, we kept the week-end business we loved, expanding it into a Christian modeling agency utilizing the students in my modeling classes at the community college.

By now, I was working a part-time job in addition to a full-time job teaching high school and giving sixty-plus hours per week to our business. I couldn't do enough to keep him happy. I loved it when he was proud of me and seemed to admire me.

After a few years we bought a two-acre home in the hills and I thought I was finally back "there" again. My husband and I were members of a church. I was helping so many people to be successful and happy. My students loved me; my clients and colleagues admired and respected me. I was internationally renowned for my fashion trend predictions and I was world-wide President of my trade association. I felt God was blessing my life. I thought this must have been why I had to go through so much suffering to get here, where I was. I was even able to work in close proximity to my children and grandchildren and was able to see them often. Life was good. I was finally "there", wealthier than I had ever dreamed in every way.

And then, God began speaking to me in my dreams and I began those sleepless nights again. I knew there was something I needed to see. I resisted looking at whatever it was so hard I been having painful stiff necks and shoulder spasms. I would try and pretend more and more that everything was okay. I was just tired. I pretended my husband and I were just too busy to have a sexual relationship. I pretended to believe it when he said he was too busy to travel and see clients with me, so I needed to go alone. I even pretended God understood when we were too busy to go to church more often than not. I pretended to myself that I was enjoying working away from home, cleaning the house, cooking, doing huge amounts of yard work, maintaining piles of student paperwork and client reports and correspondence, coaching and helping to change student's lives, training models, lecturing and on and on until I couldn't pretend any longer. I was just too tired to keep pretending.

And when my nerves broke, I began breaking into tears at my office desks, but didn't know why I was crying so hysterically. I would hide in the corner of my clothes closet and shake and tremble until I could gain some kind of control. My head and neck began to ache and my back would spasm. I believe I was caught in darkness and could not find my way out. I would cry out and ask God what was wrong. I would ask Him how I could keep serving people if that was His purpose for my life as I had come to understand it.

Finally, I asked God the questions He was waiting for. I asked Him to reveal the truth to me whatever that was; to reveal the truths as to what was happening to me. When I asked, my eyes were opened. Not all at once, but as my mind could manage it. I saw expressions on my husband's face I hadn't seen before, heard words I hadn't heard before, and noticed how often he wasn't there with me when I needed him. I realized he must be pretending too about some things, or he just didn't care. I questioned him. We would have long talks but he insisted things were okay. He did tell me that our business was being affected by my irrational moods and bad health. He said he was greatly disappointed in me and so he had decided to keep busy away from home with some architectural work again.

When I asked God for the truth, he just kept it coming. I discovered my husband was still married to his wife in Canada when we eloped and that is why we needed to be married in Mexico and he was too nervous to consummate our marriage. We were married in the church after five years, but up until that time I had supported his other family as well as work to establish him in America. He had married me to obtain his citizenship. Many other truths surfaced, but the worst truth pushed me over the edge. One night he confessed to our Bible Study Group, that included my family, that he was a gay man and had enjoyed male company often during the years he kept me so busy contributing to our extravagant lifestyle. He told us he was in a very serious relationship and had been the past three years. That was about the same time I became to troubled. God was speaking to me and was freeing me from the darkness I was caught in.

My husband's face was revealed to me as a demon that night and I could never look directly at him again without a demon appearing and his reflection glinting back at me to remind me of the truth. Satan had once again used my deep seated need for other's approval to lead me astray. Revelation 12:10 says that Satan is the accuser of the brethren...who accuses them day and night. In I Peter 5:8-9, Peter tells us to be on the alert. Your adversary, the devil, prowls about like a roaring lion, seeking someone to devour. But resist him, firm in the faith (truth). I had allowed myself to be tricked by Satan into believing I was serving Christ freely by teaching and helping others. I was so proud I was not letting anyone down, not at work, nor at home, I was actually flattered when people called me Superwoman. I was seeking the approval of everyone but God and Satan used that against me. Now I know I must reject Satan's lies about our experiences. But at that time, Satan had me caught in a web of fear, anxiety, depression and anger. I was so overwhelmed by my loss the second time, of everything in the world I had worked so hard to obtain, I nearly lost my sanity. I began having panic attacks and hyper-ventilating. I became seriously ill, oozing Satan's venom. My children were at a loss as to what to do with me. I went under psychiatric care and medication. I was even unable to help my mother when she lost her husband from cancer during that time, so she turned to more drugs and alcohol. I was lost. I was so despondent and angry; I tried to stab my husband one night while he was sleeping.

That act finally made me realize I had become an absolutely worthless person and I didn't deserve my wonderful children and their families and if I kept behaving in this way I might lose their love, too. My single motivating force to survive was a picture of my son and daughter that I clung to. I wanted them to be proud of me, yes, but most of all I did not want them to be ashamed of me as I had become of my mother. God made me see that my mother's weaknesses had become my strengths.

I struggled back to my bedroom and lay prostrate on the floor. I began to cry with deep wrenching sobs and pray to God. I prayed in this way for hours and continued into three days. All I could do was lie prostrate and pray to my Comforter and my Savior for help. I didn't want to move until I could feel the presence of the Holy Spirit again. When my time of fasting and praying was over, I knew in my heart and soul God was in control of my life once more. I asked God to forgive me for turning away from Him and seeking my worth from the approval of others. I begged forgiveness for allowing my pride and my man-pleasing motivation to become more important to me than He was. I made a heartfelt vow to God that I would give myself to Him as His servant and would encourage others to do the same. He lifted me and forgave me. And, I have kept my vow to Him. I had been caught in the devils' snare but God had brought me back. God spoke to me then and told me that He is opposed to the proud (who seek the approval of man) but gives grace to the humble (who seek the approval of God). He wants us to humble ourselves under the mighty hand of God He will lift you up at the proper time...I Peter 5:5.

Praise God!  What an awesome God He is.  He never lets go, even when we do.  How patient He is with us.

That was thirteen years ago.  I have since happily remarried and my husband and I include God in every aspect of our marriage I have been blessed with a continued career in public education and have progressed to administrative levels.  I have had many serious challenges to face and hills to climb.  Life is like that.  God never promised an easy road.  But with the God-first perspective I now have, He has richly rewarded me with more professional acclaim and recognition.  But, I have learned to give God the Glory for all that I undertake or achieve.  I thank God He has given me the wisdom, grace and strength to keep climbing in the face of adversity.  He has given me the freedom to reject Satan's enticements in the world and to stand firm on His Word on the road ahead.  This is the spiritual battle of my life.

Am I "there" yet?  I have the Peace of God which surpasses all understanding.  In 2 Thessalonians 2:4 we are assured we have been approved by God to be entrusted with the Gospel, so we speak, not as pleasing men but (pleasing) God, who examines our hearts.  I no longer seek the approval of others, only of God.  I know each man's praise will come from God when the Lord comes.

I have learned I am enough for Him, which is all I need to know.  I am God's perfect child.  He loves me and accepts me for who I am and values me among all of His children.  I would say I am "there" for now.  But I look forward with longing to the day when I will be "there" in Heaven with Him for eternity.

Made in the USA
San Bernardino, CA
20 November 2019